HOW TO STOP SMOKING WITHOUT KILLING ANYONE

BY
DAVID R. BRADLEY

How to Stop Smoking Without Killing Anyone Copyright © 2009 by David R. Bradley. Edited by Vernon Bradley and Chris McCarthy. All Rights Reserved. Printed in the United States of America. No part of this book, including designs, graphics or photographs may be reproduced or transmitted in any form or any means, electronic or mechanical, including photocopying, recording, or by any information storage or retrieval system without written permission from the author. For more information, please write David Bradley, PO Box 48, Yucaipa, CA 92399 or email: thepuravidacompany@gmail.com

TABLE OF CONTENTS

Forward

Introduction

Step 1-Stop trying to quit!
Be a smoker… admit it… be proud… do or do not… be yourself… the case for being cool vs. trying to be cool…

Step 2-You're a smoker! How did that happen?
How did you start and when was that? Why did you start? What was happening in your life at that time? What does then have to do with now? Do some math… how many have you had today? This week? This month? Year? Since starting?

Step 3-Homework
500 word essay (or more) on why you are…

Step 4-Heal your self.
Lick your wounds… passive aggressive suicide… suicide is a selfish act… forget second hand smoke, think about the people who are going to have to care for your selfish ass when you're hacking away at your lung tissue like Doc Holiday on a 3 day bender… self loathing… love for others… knowing enough about modern science to finally admit that smoking will eventually kill you…

Step 5-Positive effects of diet and exercise.
>Start using your lungs again… The science of your addiction… Nutrition to help you through the tuff times… Exercise…

Step 6-Committment
>You chose to start, now choose to stop (but don't quit)… living in the moment… minute to minute, hour to hour, day by day, week by week… always come back to now, deal with later, later… The gap between stimulus and response

Step 7-Liberation.
>Feel free to smoke and decide not to. What do you desire out of life and how are you earning it? What are you prepared to give? So you've stopped, now what?

Conclusion

Appendixes & Afterthoughts
>I can't do it… The Smokers Workout… A little on Ego… Chantix… NRT… eCigs… 5 Stages of Grief

FORWARD

By Vernon R Bradley, MA MFT and my Dad

I grew up in the forties and fifties and smoking was very suave and even romantic. In more contemporary terms, smoking was, and I guess still is for many, "cool," As a kid, I really enjoyed watching adults smoke and often bought candy cigarettes so I could also smoke. My "cigarettes" had a red tip. You know, like they were lit! I thought they looked quite real! And I knew exactly how to hold my cigarettes and how to tap them to knock off the imaginary ash!

My Godfather was a wealthy man. When he and my Godmother smoked, they used fancy cigarette holders and looked like Hollywood stars. My uncle was not so wealthy and rolled his own cigarettes, and I found that equally interesting! My Dad smoked both cigarettes and cigars. Dad could blow incredible smoke rings with cigar smoke. I would go so far as to call them magical and better than anything in the cartoons! Yes, most of the significant people in my life, rich or poor, smoked.

When I was about twelve years old, Dad introduced me to cigars. As nauseating as it was at first, I felt quite MANLY, and when my buddies would invite me into the alley to smoke cigarettes, I was quite smug in turning them down, telling them that if I wanted to smoke, I'd smoke a cigar with my Dad!

I started smoking "full time" when I was 16! Can you believe it? I smoked cigarettes, a pipe, and cigars. There was talk back then about smoking and cancer, and sometimes we referred to cigarettes as cancer sticks and coffin nails, but still the association wasn't enough to inhibit most of us smokers. But when I woke up one morning when I was twenty-four with a smoker's hack, I became a LITTLE concerned. Concerned enough to stop smoking cigarettes except on an occasion, but I jumped head on into smoking my pipes and, on special occasions, a special cigar.

I continued to smoke that occasional cigarette, my pipe, daily, and special cigars on special occasions until 1982, when I decided that it didn't make a lot of sense for a licensed therapist, who was supporting folks to become healthy, to be smoking. So I stopped.

I don't remember it being particularly difficult to stop, but what I am very very aware of is an on-going urge and craving for all three of my delights–the cigarettes, the pipe, and even the cigars. I am not hounded by the urge, but definitely haunted. And sometimes, I actually think that I could have a smoke, just for old time's sake, and get away with it. But thank God, I have resisted the fantasy! This haunting urge and craving is absolutely astonishing to me! Nicotine addiction is really powerful. It is embedded in my brain and still associated with enhancing the "romance" or the "specialness" of a given moment. Of course, that makes no sense, but that's how insidious addiction is. That's how neuropathways work, not by sense, but by connection.

I know, for other folks, stopping smoking is almost as difficult as getting off heroine. And this marvelous "little" book is for both of us, folks like myself as well as for those who suffer the throws of withdrawal and consider killing any number of innocent folks during withdrawal.

What I like most about this book is I can read and reread and be impacted each and every time. One of the feelings that come up for me is the "willies." I get the "willies" when I think about how much I smoked and how long I smoked. The "willies" help me to continue my decision to not smoke even though I am still a smoker.

What I just wrote, "I am still a smoker," is part of the profound wisdom that David offers us. He tells us to "Stop Trying To Quit.....Be a smoker!" Whoa! It's actually ancient wisdom. You never try to get rid of any part of yourself, especially the negative parts. Rather you take ownership and weave those dangling threads into the fabric of your life.

Yes, I am still a smoker. I decide each and every day NOT to smoke. The fact that I am a smoker or not makes me no better or no worse than any other human being. Wow!

How To Stop Smoking......, as you might be starting to surmise is more than an opportunity to look at your addiction to nicotine. And when you are no longer smoking (but still a smoker), you can reread and reread ***How To Stop Smoking....*** and become conscious of anything else you are "smoking" to destroy your life. It might be a lot of negative energy from people you need to get away from. It might be a belief that it's not in the cards for you to be financially successful or that you are not attractive enough to have a satisfying sexual relationship with your partner.

There are lots of different kinds of SMOKE that we inhale and sometimes insidiously get high on. And just as with the cigarettes, this other kind of negative SMOKE can invade our entire body through the production of neuropeptides which are amino acids chains specific to our emotions. So when my brain is producing "negative" neuropeptides, I find every negative thing there is to find that day. And, YES, when my brain produces "positive" neuropeptides, I find every good thing there is to find, even in the midst of a crisis. Yes, it could be that our "addiction" to these negative neuropeptides is what drove most of us into smoking in the first place. Wow!

David even touches on LOVE. Love is so interesting because it is relatively easy to love another person. The real challenge is experiencing yourself as lovable, allowing others to love you, and then loving yourself. Feeling unloved or unlovable is painful, and if there's not another human being for us to "inhale" at that moment, we will turn to that faithful friend, our addiction, whether it be nicotine, alcohol, gambling, sex, or driving your motorcycle a hundred miles an hour. Throughout the book, David invites us to learn to "love ourselves a little better" and it becomes clearer and clearer that this book is beyond stopping smoking. It's about starting to live your life. And if you want to know some simple menus to support your stopping smoking and living your life, David has included those for you as well!

I am assuming that if you are reading this Forward, you are getting ready to read further. From one smoker to another, enjoy the read. Inhale every word of it! It is wonder-filled.

INTRODUCTION

Welcome and thank you for deciding to read my book! Let me just say I have no real "qualifications" to write this book outside of the fact that I have not had a cigarette since May 21, 2002. I stopped smoking in what people call the "cold-turkey" fashion and I have not wavered, nor will I. I had tried to quit several times for several years on several occasion and failed every single time. I finally succeeded in becoming a smoker who doesn't smoke by applying the philosophies and ideals you are about to read. Many ideas I gathered from outside sources and inspirations. Some of these influencers and inspirations have been, Dr. Laura Schlessinger, Steven Covey, Grant Cardone, Napoleon Hill, and Viktor Frankl.

Another profound effect on me was September 11, 2001. The week after the attacks helped me to realize how much I wanted to live a VERY long life and how much I wanted to grow old with my then girlfriend and make her my wife. I took each day as it came and committed 100% to not smoking and this book is my story and postscript. If it helps you, excellent and congratulations. If not, thanks for reading anyway and good luck!

While you read this, I would like to encourage you to underline, write in the margins, highlight, doodle, whatever. If you want to also have a notebook or journal, might not be a bad idea. This will allow you to take notes in and put down your own thoughts and ideas for you to look back on later. Either way, dig into this material, play full out and go for it!

Also, keep in mind, there will be homework given with this book and so a personal notebook or journal set aside solely for your reading of this book might not be a bad.

You are free to read this as you wish and to gain as little or as much as possible from it.

STEP 1: STOP TRYING TO QUIT!

"Smoke em if you got em…"
-Vic Morrow

Light Up!

If you are reading this and actively smoking daily, go find yourself a nice place to sit and read. Go find someplace comfortable and quiet with good lighting and fresh air. Get settled, grab a cup of coffee or tea, make yourself at ease and then take a moment to light up a cigarette. Yes, you just read that correctly. Light up! Set down the book on how to stop smoking for a moment (just promise you'll pick it back up again) and light up a cigarette. Smoke one while you read this or any other part of this book.

Be a Smoker!

And while you're enjoying this and every other cigarette you'll smoke for the rest of your life, forget all the grief you've given yourself for smoking, forget the hard time you get from your spouse, let go of the vision of your kid looking at you weird as you light another, release the yapping you hear from your non-smoking friends and co-workers. For now and in this moment, I want you to just smoke. I want you to enjoy smoking right now in this moment and don't let anyone, *especially* yourself give you any grief about it.

BE A SMOKER!

Because here's the deal, whether you like it or not, you are a smoker! And there is nothing you or anyone else can do to take that away. You are a smoker. Stop trying to be somebody you're not and to hell with everybody else. You're a smoker, it's your body, you're life, and you can live it anyway you damn well please. In other words, the first thing you need to do right now, is to take full ownership and responsibility of and for being a smoker.

Smoking or Non? You are a smoker!

In this world there are two kinds of people. There are "Smokers" and "Non-Smokers." *You* are a smoker. These categories can be broken down into sub-categories. The sub categories can be "Smokers who smoke" and "Smokers who *do not* smoke." A smoker is someone who enjoys smoking. They like the art of smoking. Be it a cigarette, cigar, pipe, hookah, whatever. There are also smokers who've passed that part by and are hooked. They are completely addicted and are not coming back. They've accepted their fate so to speak. These are the older folks you see outside the drug store dragging a can of oxygen with one hand and having a quick "ciggie" before they go inside to pick up their prescription. You'll hear stories about someone's grandfather on his death bed dying of emphazema and practically begging for one last cigarette. If you've ever walked a row of slot machines looking for the one that's ready to burst in Vegas, you and I will be on the same page about the committed, career smoker.

There are also non-smokers who smoke. Think about that for second… You know exactly who they are. Usually a would be social-light who hangs out at the bars and in the coffee shops who will light up with a group of real smokers in the off chance they'll figure out their own identity in a blue gray nicotine haze. These are the people trying to look like they're inhaling without actually inhaling. They are awkward as hell when they hold the cigarette and also comic relief for real smokers who have made a decision to smoke.

Let go of the shame.

What's most important here for yourself as a smoker is that you recognize that smoking is a part of you and your identity. Its part of who you are now and how you are seen and if there is any shame in that, you need to let it go so you can get on with your life. You will always be a smoker in the same vein that an alcoholic is an alcoholic even if they don't drink anymore. The reasons you still smoke are yours but keep in mind that regardless of the "why", the individual that actually you are is separate from the "why". Consider this, what if, you do not smoke to be cool; what if you smoke because you already are cool. Allow me to go over that again. You do not smoke to be cool; you smoke because you are cool. Let that sink in and realize that you were cool and unique before you started smoking and will be so still even after you have decided to stop smoking.

Stop trying to quit!!!

Ok, so now what? Well, the first thing you need to do here is to stop trying to quit. What? Yes, STOP TRYING TO QUIT SMOKING! You can't quit. You're a smoker remember? You'll always be a smoker. You have yet to quit because you can't quit. It's impossible and way too hard to do. Every time you've said, "that's it no more, I'll never smoke again" you freak yourself out. Even if you get so far as to go a day or two without smoking, you'll still find yourself sitting outside a liquor store parking lot arguing with yourself. You'll be sitting there watching bums and dirty old men walk in and coming out with small brown bags of mystery. And all the while you'll be going over in your head about how you promised yourself or whichever loved one that this was it. No more! Never again! You try so hard to talk yourself out of it, only to walk inside defeated, feeling completely out of control of your behavior and you get a pack of Camels. You then try and figure out how to explain it this time. Not only to yourself, but to someone else because now you got to answer the big question: "I thought you said you were going to quit?!?!"

Don't be that guy!

Well, here's the bottom line and pardon the French but it fits. Every time you say you're going to quit and don't, you look like an asshole. That's right, an asshole. It is time to realize that you are addicted to nicotine. Your body craves it like air, food, and water. The moment you say, "I quit" you think "Oh my god I'll never smoke again" and you're craving a cigarette even if you just finished one.

The Popeye/Yoda Condition

The idea here is what I would call the Popeye/Yoda Condition. We all know who Popeye is right? There's a slight chance you don't know who Yoda is and if that's the case, you are here-be ordered to not allow the year to end without watching *Star Wars, The Empire Strikes Back,* and *Return of the Jedi.* Watch them in that order and feel free to smoke while watching them.

SIDEBAR: *If you're reading this on December 31st preparing for a glorious New Year's Resolution, then it's OK to shelve the Star Wars Trilogy till later in January.*

But I totally digress, here's the point. Popeye said what? "I yam what I yam!" Right? And Yoda said, "Do or do not, there is no try!" Exactly! And that goes for you too. An individual cannot change a behavior or habit until first he owns it and accepts responsibility for it. That is why for now you should be smoking and enjoying it and thumbing your nose (feel free to use a different finger and leave out the nose) at anyone who tells you otherwise.

I (state your name) am a smoker.

Smoke or do not smoke. Stop trying to quit. Give yourself a break. Have a smoke and a yellow smile. Most importantly, stop beating your head against a wall and living in your self-imposed world of shame and guilt.

STEP ONE: STOP TRYING TO QUIT!

HOMEWORK:

Set the book down for a minute. Take a break to digest the information. Write down in your notebook or in the pages provided, anything that just stirred up for you while you were reading. Even if you think it's not relevant (trust me, it is, so write it down and explore the thought!) What did you read here that got your wheels turning? What did you see that reminded you of you? Where are you at with your addiction? Next, when you're ready, go back and read some more.

_____
_____
_____
_____
_____
_____
_____

STEP 2: YOU'RE A SMOKER! HOW DID THAT HAPPEN?

"Those who do not know their history, are doomed to repeat it"
—A bunch of dead guys, but most likely, George Santayana

You're hooked!

The next and important step in stopping smoking is to look at the "how's" and the "why's" of your addiction. Trust me, you're addicted. If you weren't, you wouldn't be reading this nor would you have just said "I'm not an addict!" Yeah, yeah, yeah, we've heard it all before, you're in complete control, you can quit anytime you want and so on and so forth. You're so right!

Be a Newsie and a Dick!

It also helps to look at the "when" and the "where." You'll have to look at this part of yourself and circumstance as a reporter or a detective. This does not mean you'll be confronting your inner child or that you'll be doing an exercise where you're going to find yourself rocking a pillow labeled "self" and apologizing for abusing it in some a small pool of tears and suppressed anger. There will be no pop-psych here. Just real talk and opinion.

In the first step, we took ownership of being a smoker. This is a very important step in what very well may become the most important decision of your life so far. Now, in this step we will examine the who, what, when, where, how, and why of our habit. We're going to use this part of the book as a work book, so get ready to start jotting down some thoughts and ideas here.

Write down the first time you remember smoking. Write:

The first time I remember smoking was:

_____
_____
_____

After that, write down what it was like? That first cigarette was like:

_____
_____
_____
_____

How did you feel?

The first time I smoked a cigarette I felt:

_____

_____

_____

How did you get it?

Here's how I got a hold of my first cigarette…

_____

_____

_____

See if you can see yourself having that first cigarette.

I can see myself smoking my first cigarette. My surroundings looked like...

_____

_____

_____

Spend some time with this and get back to the book in a while.

Feel free to smoke while you're doing this too.

The next thing you'll want to figure out is WHY.

Why did you pick up that first cigarette? Why did you do it?

I decided to have my first cigarette because:

_____

_____

_____

Why was it so appealing?

I was attracted to this cigarette because:

_____

_____

What was happening in your life at that time?

In my life at that time:

_____
_____

How old were you?

I was…

_____

When did you start buying them?

I bought my first pack when:

_____
_____

When did smoking go from once in a while to habit to addiction for you?

_____
_____

Finally write about why you continued to smoke.

I kept smoking because…

_____
_____
_____
_____
_____
_____
_____

Know your history.

For now, you don't have to worry about now... Huh? Look, the point of these exercises is to understand your history and take a look at your past. We all know the saying about history. If you don't know your history, you are doomed to repeat it. And so it goes with smoking. One must have a grasp on their personal story and know what smoking means to them before they can decide to let it go. Have you ever been lost or lost something? What do you do more often than not? That's right, retrace your steps. That's what we're doing here. Because, the reality here is as smokers in this day and age, we may just be a little lost, wouldn't you agree? I mean, c'mon now, what year is it? If you're still smoking, then you are in one hell of a dysfunctional relationship! Sure on one hand it relaxes you; gives you joy, and makes you feel cool. Also, smoking is a nice condiment to sex, drugs, booze, music, food, film, you name it and a cigarette goes well with anything.

But on the other hand, it's killing you. Literally, it's shortening your life span. So, if you want to move forward, it's very important to know where you were and how you got there. Once that knowledge exists and is present for you to look at and analyze, you are then empowered to make a new road map and take off in the new direction of your choosing. The past cannot repeat itself unless you allow it to do so.

The past cannot repeat itself unless you allow it to do so.

See what I did there...

It is also important to know your history so you can separate from it. You can decide to take a "that was then, this is now" approach. You can decide to take on an attitude of "*regardless* of then, this is now." TODAY. You are *NOT* your past or future but *your* present. Your actions in the present time are the only actions you have any direct and immediate control over.

HOMEWORK AGAIN:

Are you ready to do a little math? This is information that will act like a garnish. It's inspiring, yet not that motivating. Well, maybe it is motivating. That will be up to you!

How many cigarettes have you had today? Write that in your workbook or notebook. Do it now.

Next write how many you had yesterday…

Finish the following:

I smoke ___ cigarettes a day.

Multiply that by seven and write: I smoke ___ cigarettes a week.

Multiply that by 4 and write: I smoke ___ cigarettes a month.

Then multiply that by 12 and write: I smoke ___ cigarettes a year.

Then multiply that number by how many years you've been smoking and write:

I have smoked ___ cigarettes in my life so far.

Now take your age and add 20. Multiply that number by your annual cigarettes and write:

If I live to the age of ___ I will have smoked ___ cigarettes.

Now put that in your pipe and...

Well, you'll know what to do.

I know what I did. I started this book! I came up with all kinds of plans and none worked. I kept *trying* to quit. I tried weaning off a week at a time. I was at a pack and a half a day. So I said this week, only twenty-nine cigarettes. Next week, twenty-eight. The week after, twenty-seven and so forth. I think I got down to 15 a day and that was still 5475 cigarettes a year. Or 16,425 minutes saved in my life.

The reality was, in no time, I was back to a pack a day. I went to the nicotine gum for a while, but it didn't do it. It helped with the nicotine craving but I still wanted to inhale more than air. I remember in college one year a buddy of mine and I decided to quit smoking tobacco products. We made a bet. First one to smoke a cigarette owes the other guy a hundred bucks. Well, we never said we wouldn't smoke, we just said no cigarettes. So, I was stoned for about 47 days if memory serves me. It was probably less. More like a week and a half, it just *felt* like 47 days. Finally, we broke down and had a tobacco cigarette. Neither one of us forked over the hundred bucks.

Another smart move.

Eventually, I switched to "all natural" cigarettes. Why? So I can get "all natural" cancer? What kind of idiot worries about whether his cigarette is all-natural or not? Or if the filter is bio-degradable? Give me a break. How about not smoking and polluting the air and your lungs? To hell with the filter. I guess some smoke is worse than others.

Ironically, with the "naturals" I smoked a little less frequently and after a month or so, my "nic-fits" weren't as bad as when I was on name-brand cigarettes. So I think I might have given myself a leg up, but I'm not convinced. I'm fairly certain that was all in my head. At the end of the day though, it will come down to a minute-by-minute decision that we are going to cover in a later chapter.

The deal with me.

My story as a smoker came early. My grandfather smoked cigars. Everyone in my mom's family smoked cigarettes. I used to love the smell. I also remember my mother putting vanilla extract on cotton balls and leaving them around the house to eliminate the smell after my folks had friends over. In the seventies, everybody smoked. I remember the ads. I remember seeing adults do it and I couldn't wait to do it myself. My dad smoked a pipe. Wow just like Sherlock Holmes. My dad looked cool with that pipe in his bathrobe. A real Playboy type. Then there was this teenage girl up the street who smoked and she was cool. She'd swipe them from her mom. My best friend's neighbor's mom smoked those Moore 100's with the brown paper. She was cool in a sort of Hill Billy Bette Davis sort of way.

What I remember most from the seventies was that the sixties were over and that the eighties hadn't started. Everything was in transition. And smoking wasn't quite yet on its way out. It seemed everyone was starting to get the idea that this may not be such a good idea after all but I didn't care. All I knew was that come adulthood, I'm a smoker.

In seventh or eighth grade I came down with some kind of asthma. It kicked in after a really bad cold and lasted for a year or two. I remember having an attack at school one day and in a panic, not being able to breathe and at the same time having a terrible coughing fit, I started to climb a fence, trying to get higher and higher, hoping that I could get air up there. I almost passed out from the panic. All the other kids were staring at me and the yard duty was yelling at me to calm down and all I wanted was a breath of fresh air! That incident happened at least 4 times at various points in that eighth grade year.

My asthma or whatever it was cleared up by mid-summer before high school. So I tried out for the cross-country team because my dad had joined the jogging craze and it seemed like a sport I could play. I wasn't very good at team sports so here was my chance. I ran my best but my lungs were weak and I hated it. By the time I started high school I was sneaking a cigarette or two a week. Not really committed to the "inhale" yet but I loved feeling older. I quit running in favor of the theatre and dabbled in a smoke or two every now and again, knowing that it was really just a matter of "when" not "if" I would start smoking.

By my junior year, most of my friends smoked and it was cool. I remember making out with this girl who smoked regularly and the flavor of Marlboro lights on her tongue turned me on. I was hooked and I had not even really started. The idea was more compelling than anything.

The real seduction however, came from one man. Humphrey Bogart. Bogie was it. In Bogie I found a fast-talking, strong, confident man who was good with the ladies and tuff with the fellas. Everything I was not. I was weak, insecure, and not real good with the ladies. I was very shy with people in the beginning until I warmed up to you, felt safe, and then I could open up.

I found some of my strength in the theatre at Yucaipa High School but wanted more and Bogie was it. I also fell in love with history and that era. The 20's through JFK. If America had any innocence left to lose it was when we lost JFK. (How funny,

I say "we" as if I was there. I was born in 72! That's how powerful my connection with the past is!) Anything before that had my attention. I fell in love with the gangster movie and the mafia, I fell in love with Phillip Marlow and Sam Spade, Bogie and Bacall, it was sheer magic and I yearned for a time machine. Naturally, I started smoking officially somewhere after renting Casablanca for the first time. "Now Voyager" was like icing on the cake, Paul Henreid lighting two cigarettes, one for him and the other for Betty Davis and the smoke rising on the screen from the ashtray. I just couldn't take it anymore. Bogart was in me and I knew with enough practice I could be that cool. Little did I realize I was that cool to begin with and I didn't need a cigarette to bring that cool out. But, when you're seventeen, a cigarette sure helps. It was all downhill from there.

On December 30, 1990 at 12:01am, my eighteenth birthday, I hopped into my parent's car, drove the 3 blocks to 7-11 and proudly bought a Playboy magazine, a lottery ticket, and my first legal pack of camel non-filters. The son of a bitch behind the counter didn't even ask for my ID. If I'd have known that was coming I'd have thrown in a fifth of Jack Daniel's. Oh well,

I didn't care all that much. All I knew was I was officially a smoker. Finally!

So, what was all that math and writing about for earlier? Was it for guilt? What about stirring up some shame? Was it to be cruel? No, it was designed to begin your inner dialogue. It's all food for your thought. This is information for you. You will sift through it so you can ask your own questions. Learn your history and get it out there so you can separate from it and then make a decision to move forward.

Currently, it's holding you back. You can let it go instead of carrying it with you the whole time, everywhere you go and bringing you down.

STEP 3: EVEN MORE HOMEWORK

"All truths are easy to understand once they are discovered, the point is to discover them"
-Galileo

Try this on like a jacket.

In this little chapter you will have an assignment.

For many of us, life is truly about cause and effect. I believe this is sad because there is so much more to us as humans then we give ourselves credit for. I am just as guilty of this as the next guy! Earlier I mentioned looking at yourself like a detective. Now, I want you to be like a doctor. And a *good* doctor at that. A good doctor treats the cause, not the symptom. So much of modern medicine is invested in treating symptoms and ignoring what the symptom is telling you. Look at the common cold. How many variations of that little strain of whatever are out there? Zillions, right? And how many versions of the exact same cold medicine are sold daily? Zillions. All treating the runny nose, stuffy nose, cough, fever, headache and so on. If you and the whole world started examining why they just caught a cold in the first place instead of treating all the symptoms, ultimately, I think there'd be less people calling in sick. When you get sick, it's your body telling you, "Hey, I'm a little run down here. So run down, I can't fight off this little bugger that's invading us right now and so I'm going put you down for a few days while I handle it." You must look at why you got sick and address that.

Look at what the media does. The media railroads you all day with negativity, death, pain, illness and all that is wrong with the world. They want you to feel weak and helpless. Then they hit you with a commercial for an antidepressant. How many medication commercials are there?

I know what you're thinking again, what does this have to do with smoking, right? I'll tell you. If you invest your valuable time on this planet treating your symptoms, you'll never cure the "cold" in your heart. You will keep on repeating the same behaviors and you'll continue asking yourself, "Why does this always seem to happen to me?" A symptom is a sign from your body. It's like getting constructive criticism or feedback and its right from the source. Listen to your body and pay attention to what it is trying to tell you and teach you. Symptoms are your opportunity to examine yourself and make a needed correction, develop into something better, stronger and more human. Smoking is a symptom of something and that's what I'd like you to examine now.

I'd like you to write a 500 word (or more) essay entitled: **Why I am trying to kill myself?**

Come again? No, you read that right. Think about it. You can't deny that it's bad for you. The evidence is overwhelming. Sure there are exceptions, but what are the odds that *you* won't die from a smoking related illness? And so if you're going that route, I'm guessing you'd be the first person to sign up for the team if Russian Roulette became an Olympic Sport.

I remember while I was actively smoking reading an article in a magazine about a 100 plus year old woman in France who quit smoking when she was 90! I remember thinking to myself,"OK, see, it is possible, you can still smoke and not get sick." I was relieved for a while. Then I realized that I'm *me* and not this little old French lady who can smoke for 70 years. I need to look at me and my symptoms, both physically and emotionally if I'm going to stop and stay stopped.

Now please don't think that I'm saying to go open up every old wound and simmer on why your life is miserable. There's no need to dwell on how you were abused or that nobody loves you!

Rather, what I'm suggesting here is that you rummage around in the back rooms of your mind until you find that belief that tells you over and over that you do not deserve a quality of life better than what you have right now. I'm asking you to ponder that idea and also address your own mortality and how you want to live out the rest of your life. Forget your past for now because that's all it is. You can't go back.

However, you can look forward and figure out why you hold on to this belief.

Are you are mad at yourself for something? Do you feel guilty about something that probably wasn't really your fault? Or maybe it was, so what! Are you going to make yourself pay until you die?

Do you have a sense of little or no worth? What is it that's causing you to hate and punish yourself? Is that even what you are actually doing by smoking or is it something else? Ponder on it. Then ponder some more. Write about it. Go…

I am trying to kill myself by smoking because:

Hold on… Don't start writing yet… hold on one second…

SIDEBAR: A brief note to those of you who are shaking your head right now and thinking that writing an essay like this is juvenile and stupid because that's "just not me". If you're thinking, I love life and enjoy smoking and I'll quit when I quit, I am not trying to slowly kill myself, who is this guy kidding, I'm not going to write about that…"

Here's my 2 cents on that. Please turn the page...

WAKE THE #$*%$ UP!!!

Now start writing…

STEP 4-HEAL YOUR SELF.

*"True healing requires a new way of life –
in combination with insight and profound
psychological transformation."
-Dan Millman*

Lick your wounds.

By now if you followed the directions, you've got some ideas on how you are living or not living your life. You also got a small examination into your personal history. It is time now to heal and more importantly time to move forward. Here is the thing about your past. The good things from your past and the bad things are there to stay. You cannot make them go away no matter how hard you try. And when I mean the past, I'm not just talking about 10 years ago. I'm talking about 5 seconds ago too. If it's happened, you can't change it so don't give it too much power over your *new* decisions and certainly don't allow it to affect the next 5 seconds or 10 years.

"You are powerful beyond measure." - Marianne Williamson

What is important to recognize is your own power in life. More importantly, to recognize the power you have over *you* in particular. Start using your power by recognizing it is time to give yourself permission to forgive yourself for all the stupid shit you've done.

Remember, the past is there in the shadows trying to influence your future. Perhaps our shadowy past is synonymous with our ego.

Ultimately, it is up to us, not our ego, to decide whether or not we're going to allow the foolish things, stupid things, unfortunate things, tragic things, or horrible things to control a future that has yet to be written.

Also, it is vital that you recognize that you and only you write your future. What happens all around you - not in your control. What you do about what happens all around you, TOTALLY in your control.

A perfect example of this is the traffic jam. Assuming you're not the cause of the traffic jam, here you find yourself on the way to somewhere and bam! Traffic jam! Now some people actually think that by honking their horn the problem will resolve faster and some of those people even believe that if they push harder *on* the horn that the horn actually gets louder there by increasing the rate at which "these idiots will get out of my way."

Let's take a look at that shall we? You're stuck in traffic. Now what? This situation is out of your control. What you do have control over is how you respond to the traffic and the people around you. Just so you know, I've been that guy. I hate traffic with a passion and I live in Los Angeles. I hate L.A. drivers and I hate the whole hurry up and wait attitude. However, I have a lot of books on tape and getting stuck in traffic is now a perfect opportunity to just stop. Listen to that song you love, toss in a CD on anger management and get to work, learn a language, listen to that book you've always wanted to read.

I realized that when stuck in traffic the people in these car suddenly ceased being humans and became obstacles. That's no way to live and no way to see people.

You can't always control what happens around you, but you certainly have a very good shot at what you decide to do about it. That one is a life long journey, but practice it and it gets better and easier with time.

If you'd like to plug this into the big picture, take a look at people like Helen Keller, Stephen Hawking and Christopher

Reeve and see how they've responded to *their* situation.

Blast from the past.

So, now let's get back to your past. It is perfectly all right to forgive yourself for doing stupid stuff. Stop letting it dictate your future. If you've been a victim of circumstance, let go of any guilt you may have about it. And don't think you don't. You may not recognize it or see it, but it's there and you got it so find it and let it go. If your ego is running rampant in your life then this may be a hard concept to grasp. I'll touch on ego later, but for now what *is* important is that you give yourself permission to let go of your past and focus on moving forward and staying in *this* moment of your life because this is the only moment that truly exists!

Tirade

While you wrestle with this concept, let's go back to your essay. With all the research and evidence out there you cannot deny that smoking is bad for you. Over 400,000 people die **each year** from smoking related illness. I could go on and on about it but as I was researching the internet to get some hard evidence to throw in your face, I realized how trite that would be and how I as the writer here do not under any circumstances want to even remotely come across as some Rob Reiner super liberal anti-smoking advocate. I saw a web site that was "dedicated to protecting the rights of non-smokers." When I read that, I almost puked on my keyboard. I haven't had a cigarette in several years and that quote alone has resulted in a craving so strong I'm beside myself. I feel like running to a liquor store and buying a pack of Camel non-filters and making my way to some posh Santa Monica restaurant and smoke the whole pack! The rights of non-smokers? What about the smoker? Kicked out of restaurants. OK, that makes some sense. But these ding-dongs trying to ban smoking in public outdoor places like parks and sidewalks. That has got to stop. If a person doesn't like the smell... MOVE! It's reverse discrimination! I or any other individual has as much right *to* smoke as another has a right to *not* smoke. I mean can't we all just get along? Second hand smoke kills who? Aside from the old man in the commercial who lost his wife, where are the rest of the bodies? How many headstones do you see that read "lost to second hand smoke." Give me a break!

Ban smoking! Come on. Can't we just set aside areas where smoking is permitted? I mean bars? No smoking in bars? I can't have a cigarette with a glass of whiskey? What's the point? I mean if I or anybody else is going down then they should be allowed to go down as big as they want! No, I've got to step outside the bar to smoke. I wouldn't want all those folks with liver disease to get second hand lung cancer. This is the United States of America! Tobacco was the commodity that secured this great nations financial independence. We as Americans should show it a little more respect…

Attention readers:
The rant you have just been exposed to is a fine example of nicotine's hold on the human psyche even in several years post exposure. Nicotine is a highly addictive substance that should not be taken lightly. We now return you to your regularly scheduled "How to Stop Smoking Without Killing Anyone" reading experience.

So, where was I? Ah yes, smoking is bad, mmm-k? (If you watch South Park, that was funny, if you don't watch South Park, just know that to those that do, it was) Smoking will either kill you outright or lead to other things that will kill you and yes, we are all going down either way. I understand the whole thing about death and taxes.

However, the point here is quality of life. So, let's look at that for a moment.

Smoking can greatly increase your quality of life. Smoking is pleasurable. It goes well with anything. It's romantic, sexy, relaxing, classy, etc. Smoking also stinks (to other people – I love the smell personally, still do), it decreases your lung capacity, kills your taste buds, wrinkles your skin, erodes your voice, etc. So, now what? Time to face the cold hard fact that eventually you will die as a result of this little dried up plant rolled up in thin paper.

So, do you want to die at a ripe old age or check out in your mid-fifties or early sixties, (maybe sooner) in extreme pain and discomfort? You do want to grow old with your loved ones and watch your family grow and blossom right? For those of you without family, quit screwing around and get your life together!

The first step is to release yourself of the bonds of addiction. Smoking is (and don't think it's not) a passive aggressive form of suicide and self-mutilation. That is what I realized and hung on to and still do.

Nicotine releases serotonin in the brain which makes you feel happy. So when I wasn't happy or wanted to prolong my content or enhance it, I'd smoke. Simply put most of the time I wasn't happy and when I was happy, I wasn't happy enough. How pathetic is that? More, more, more!

SIDEBAR: *There nothing wrong with more. It's just more of what? Follow?*

More? That's your ego running you around. The next thing you know, since smoking will kill you and you are smoking then it's pretty simple to conclude that you are slowly trying to kill yourself.

However most likely, if you, like me, haven't fully realized this and you're not too keen on jumping off a bridge or hanging yourself in the back yard. You're probably not too interested in parking yourself in the garage with a bottle of whiskey, the car in neutral and the window cracked either. Really, you're not into that or any other creative expression of selfish self-loathing you can think of.

So what do you do instead of snacking on a bottle of Unisom with a bottle of Smirnoff to wash it down? You smoke! That's right, you smoke your little heart out.

Eventually, you'll get what you're after. Confirmation that this world is never going to give you what you truly want. And why? I may be because you're either too scared to let go of whatever it is from your past that is holding you back and keeping you there or you may feel so connected to it, you don't know what you'd do without it.

You also, very well may have convinced yourself that you are not worthy of any real and natural joy, love, peace, or happiness. You might not believe you deserve waking up in the morning happy to be alive and without a cough. Consequently, anytime you get a shot at real happiness happening, you find a way to undermine it so you can then supplement the real deal with artificial means such as cigarettes.

These little cancer sticks are the last thing to go. After drugs and alcohol, it's the last one to overcome. I believe it's the 13th step. Caffeine is the 14th Step, but that's a whole other book!

So for those of you in the program or are familiar with it at all, after step twelve which is about spiritual awakening and a compounding decision to carry the other 11 steps to the world and alcoholics plus the promise to practice the steps, the next best thing to do is rid yourself of addiction all together. Step up to the plate of exercising your free will and choose to live fully in the moment you have and tie each moment together into a life of purpose and meaning. Must give credit where credit is due:

"Time is limited, so I better wake up fresh every morning and know that I have just one chance to live this particular day right and to string my days together into a life of action and purpose."
-Lance Armstrong.

These are the quotes that stick with you day in and day out, the ones that nag at you when you crap out.

I'd suggest writing this down and putting it next to your toilet so you'll see it daily and often. Some may see it more than others but I'm sure you get my point!

"Time is limited, so I better wake up fresh every morning and know that I have just one chance to live this particular day right and to string my days together into a life of action and purpose."
-Lance Armstrong.

STEP 5 - THE POSITIVE EFFECTS OF DIET AND EXERCISE.

"Strength does not come from winning. Your struggles develop your strengths. When you go through hardships and decide not to surrender, that is strength."
-Arnold Schwarzenegger

Exercise saved my life!

Exercise is something that has helped me tremendously. The key here is to start using your lungs for something other than smoking. Even while I smoked, I still went to the gym. As a kid, I was small and weak and consequently, got picked on... a lot. In between 7th and 8th grade, I picked up weightlifting at the local community college. Granted, I had no clue what to do or how to do it and there was no one to really coach me. I had to get all my training knowledge from muscle mags. Fortunately, I had definitely found something I could do and have that was mine with no one to put me down. I got a little muscular and my confidence went up. By High School weightlifting was my hobby and I always looked forward to the next time I could get into a gym. Lifting weights is great for anyone. It is self-competition. Any individual can get into a gym and track their own progress and set attainable goals and develop their body.

My suggestion for a routine as a "Soon-To-Be-Not-Smoking-Right-Now-Smoker" is to begin a light cardiovascular workout... wait... hold on... legal jargon:

> As with all exercise programs before beginning any exercise and nutrition program it is highly recommended that you consult with your physician.

Just a little bit at first!

Ok, sorry about that. Anyway, a light cardio program of brisk walking with a little jogging thrown in there wouldn't hurt. Work up to more jogging than walking. Start doing things that make you breath deep and crave oxygen. If jogging is out of the question, bike, jump rope, swim, anything that gets your heart pumping, blood flowing, and (most importantly in the beginning) shortens your breath. Shortening your breath will be like a preview.

Try this: Go outside and run until you can't breathe. Then imagine being that out of breath just trying to walk to the bathroom.

The reason is your lungs are clogged with tar and smoke and your body can't absorb oxygen like it used to. This is where you're headed. The beautiful thing though is that your body has a tremendous ability to self-correct and heal. It is possible to increase and recover a large amount if not all of your lung capacity.

Commit to spending 30 minutes a day on exercise. After a 15-20 minute walk/jog do some stretching and light calisthenics. Try 100 jumping jacks, 25 push-ups, 10 pull-ups, 50 sit-ups, or 50 leg-raises. Do those numbers look too high for you? Then do what you can. Even if it's only one of each! What if you worked up to these numbers? Would you feel a major since of accomplishment? Would you be significantly healthier? What if you did this even if you're still smoking? Chances are if you can do something like this you may lose interest in smoking all together.

Let's say you can't exercise. Let's say you're either too old or infirmed or sick or impaired somehow. Whatever! The next thing I want you to do is to go out and join a gym. Get in there and workout. There is no excuse for not exercising! Even if it's just a little bit. Sit in your wheel chair and curl soup cans if you have to. The key here is getting healthier! Figure it out!

Look, you remember when you were a kid and you'd run around and get out of breath? Remember the rush you got from running really, really fast? I used to run on the beach as a kid. During the summer our family would spend a week or two in Shell Beach, California. We'd drive out to Pismo and I'd run my butt off. I'd get right up against the water and go. I would run as fast and as hard as I possibly could. It felt like flying. It felt as if at any moment I would lift off with the seagulls and soar. I skipped that activity for almost 15 years and have recently picked it up again and my God it feels great!

Exercise releases all kinds of feel-good chemicals in your brain. It releases endorphins and serotonin. It makes you feel good especially if you hit a peak level and are able to go beyond that. When you hit a level you've never been to before, it's exhilarating.

Smoking, mind you, also makes us feel good. It comforts us, sooths us, makes us feel happy, and the price tag for this is monstrous. Shortened life span with a really piss poor exit strategy. Exercise will do all of the good stuff, extend your lifespan and not kill you. So my advice to you is to not just give it a try, but to make a commitment to doing some level of exercise. It will help. Regardless of your current fitness level, the beauty of it is that you can always improve and strengthen your body.

Obsession maybe?

When the fitness bug bites and it takes a firm hold on you consider yourself blessed. To aid you on your quest, I recommend reading three books. The first one is *"The Education of a Bodybuilder"* by Arnold Schwarzenegger. This book is inspiring in so many ways. It shows what true drive is and what real motivation and hunger is. This book will help you in all aspects of life and get you "pumped." There are also some very sound exercise routines and nutrition programs for you to consider.

SIDEBAR: If you're as disappointed as I am in Arnold's behavior of late, read this book anyway. It's not about him now, rather it's about what you can be.

The next book is *"Body for Life"* by Bill Phillips. This is a great book for a solid exercise/fitness lifestyle that is built around improving on your current fitness level, growing and developing your inner as well as outer strength. Detailed routines and nutrition that are simple and highly effective. I should know, I've done the *"Body For Life"* challenge twice.

The final book I recommend is *"Power to the People"* by Pavel Tsatouline. This is an amazing book. It's old school weightlifting for a modern age. I'm talking turn of the century bicycle mustache strong man type of stuff. What's so good about this book is that it shows the basics of strength. Not just physical strength either. This is the kind of strength that will filter into the rest of your life and improve your overall wellbeing. Following this program not only made me strong in body, but in mind and spirit as well.

Any of these books will benefit you greatly in your quest to stop smoking and become a better, stronger, healthier human.

Currently, I'm using Russian Kettlebells for my exercise. Basically a Kettlebell looks like a giant cannonball with a thick handle.

Let me just tell you, if you're in decent shape already and you want to stop smoking, get hooked on Kettlebell lifting. 90% of all Kettlebell exercises do not mix well with a smoke infested lung. Kettlebells will get the heart pumping and is an ideal way to get you sucking wind. Hands down, Kettlebell lifting has been the best thing that ever happened to my body and I guarantee if you give it a shot, you'll find an incredibly healthy addiction.

You also can check out *RichMansGym.com*. This is an amazing resource for practical and tactical home-based strength and conditioning. If you're not a gym rat and are interested in a more unconventional way of developing the strength and endurance of a Spartan warrior, that is a great website to visit.

What goes down the hatch.

On the matter of diet and nutrition, just eat well. C'mon, you know that a "#1 combo" with a diet coke for breakfast is not going to cut it. I'm not saying its rice cakes and brussel sprouts for the rest of your life, but I am saying it's time to start feeding your body quality food. Drop the burger and fries combo at the local easiest to get to fast food establishment and replace that with something healthy. Heathy foods that will help you rebuild your body and flush out the toxins. Have more salads, fresh vegetables and healthy fats. Eat quality food. Your body deserves it. Eat lean meats, easy to digest proteins, lots of veggies, and high fiber foods. Make it a point to avoid processed white sugar and white flour products. Substitute sweet potatoes for regular potatoes, use honey in your coffee if you have to sweeten it, drink 1% or skim milk, use whole grain whole wheat breads. You know what to do. If you don't, *really* don't, see the "Stop Smoking Diet" at the end of this chapter.

Water

Your body is made up mostly of water, so eat foods that have a lot of water in them and drink a lot of water. You should be drinking 10-15 full glasses of water a day. Personally, I drink 240 ounces of water a day. That's 15 glasses, assuming the glass is 16 ounces. Our body is 70% water! DRINK IT! No debate here. Just do it.

Nutritional supplements

Multi-vitamins, antioxidants! Get a multi-vitamin and take it. Make sure to take one in the morning and one in the evening. Cigarettes deplete the body of many nutrients. The major ones are Vitamin A, Vitamins C, E, and B-complex (especially B12), Beta-carotene, Folic acid, Zinc, and Selenium. It is important to replace these micronutrients. Even if you never stop smoking, you should still exercise and get on a multi-vitamin.

The other big concern for so many people when they stop smoking is the withdrawal phase. I read somewhere that an individual has better odds of getting off heroin, than nicotine. I don't know if that's actually true or not, but the implication is scary especially when there was all that talk in the '90's about the tobacco companies spiking their product with MORE nicotine. So for the moment, let's take a look at nicotine addiction and what nicotine is.

Know your enemy

Why? In battle, one must know their opponent. If you are going to STOP, not quit, your body will fight you, hence the withdrawals. Therefore, if you know what's coming and why, you can be better prepared for it.

Nicotine is an alkaloid. It occurs within nature and is made up of carbon, nitrogen, hydrogen and oxygen. Nicotine, as you already know, has a wonderful little stimulating effect on the body. FYI, caffeine is also an alkaloid. No wonder coffee and cigarettes go together so well!

Tobacco and nicotine have been used for hundreds if not thousands of years as a mood altering substance. Nicotine makes up about 5% of the tobacco plant itself and when you smoke you ingest about .5 - 1mg per cigarette. A normal cigarette has about 10-20mg of nicotine in it.

Now are you ready for the kicker?

Pullout 3 cigarettes and look at them. If you extracted all the nicotine in those 3 "cigies" and converted it into a liquid form and then knocked it down your gullet like Dean Martin on his birthday, you would drop dead…

Let me run that by you one more time, because I'm thinking about the cartoon type of scene where you go rigid and fall to one side with the "X's" over your eyes. Chew on this for a moment! 60mg of nicotine in one shot is FATAL! To help put this into perspective for you, one ounce of liquid is equal to 28,349.52 milligrams. It only takes 60mg of nicotine to straight up and kill you dead. D. E. A. D. Dead.

So, when you take a drag or a hit, the nicotine has a stimulating effect on the central nervous system. Adrenaline kicks in which means your blood pressure and heart rate elevate. Nicotine also affects your metabolism, body temperature, muscle tension and even some hormones. Ironically, all this stuff going on in your body is perceived as a pleasurable feeling. The other grand irony is that your body in its quest for homeostasis adapts. So now in order to get that pleasurable feeling again you need MORE. Hurray! More! And so do you know what that means? Gottcha! Another notch on Big Tobacco's bed post!

Congratulations, you are now addicted to nicotine because in order for you to feel the new normal you've created, you need to smoke more.

Personally, I was at a pack a day before I knew it. Then it was two. I downshifted to a pack and a half and held that course for a while. Then I would bounce back between half a pack a day to a pack and a half. It all depended on the day. Either way, I was hooked and coming back would **not** be easy.

So now, your brain has been rewired by the nicotine. Yes, rewired. The rewiring has created a new "normal" for your brain.

Your body needs to feel normal. I was trying to read the specifics of how that works and trying to translate it into English so it would make sense to you all readers out there and here's what I came up with.

Nicotine, like heroin and cocaine, rewires your brain. Nicotine makes your brain function differently and so in order for you to feel "normal", you crave it like you would crave water and food.

In many respects, our brain functions like a computer. It processes, stores and uses information. Nicotine changes the way your brain processes, stores and uses information. It changes the way it functions. For example, nicotine will attach itself to certain receptors in the brain that effect muscle control, energy level, heart rate, and breathing. It also affects how you process information as well as learning and memory.

The other "interesting" effect of nicotine is the relationship it has with the release of dopamine. When you smoke, dopamine is released in the reward pathways of your brain. This is the same dopamine that is released after you eat food, drink water, and perform other necessary functions for survival. Are you with me so far? Are you starting to get it? Your brain now believes it needs nicotine to survive. How this all works technically is beyond me. Just stick with bottom line on this one.

Nicotine is bad and enough nicotine will leave you chemically dependent!

Once hooked and when the flow of nicotine is interrupted, you begin to experience withdrawals. These are most unpleasant and can drive you up the wall. Literally, I wanted to crawl up the walls. Why? Well, as previously mentioned, your brain now needs it to survive, or so you think. Your brain and body needs to maintain "normal" or return to its original state, so to speak. This takes me back to when I was trying to climb the fence in the school yard in the hopes of getting more air.

What this also reminds me of is in the movie "The Abyss" when Ed Harris is going to dive to the bottom of the ocean and the suit they put him in has liquid oxygen. He now has to re-learn to breath a liquid as we all did when we were in our mother's womb. So in this scene, every instinct in his body told him if he inhales this liquid, he will drown. The same is true for the smoker without a cigarette. I'll die without it. The feeling is like drowning. This is why it is so hard for people to stop and in my opinion, impossible to "quit."

However, like drowning, once you take that breath and accept your fate, they say it's peaceful. Go figure!

Withdrawal symptoms as you probably already know include, irritability, anxiety, and depression. For me, the worst part was the desire to inhale smoke. To take a nice long drag, inhale and then exhale that beautiful aroma. Even as I write this, the desire slips back. To light up and take that drag… in the words of Colonel Frank Slade, "…who-ra…"

Addiction

This brings up addiction in general. According to Wikipedia, The Free Encyclopedia online, addiction can be defined as, and "a compulsion to repeat behavior regardless of its consequences." Isn't *that* interesting? Especially how now in this day and age, unless you've been living under a rock, we all know how bad smoking is, yet we do it anyway. We do it anyway because we are addicted.

Addicted to what? Well for some it's the nicotine, the chemicals. For others it's the habit, the oral fixation, the hand-to-mouth motion. For most, it's a complex web of multiple habits, mental imagery, and physical addiction. Withdrawals can be a bear. Mostly it's the need to inhale more than air that drives you wild. At least that's how it was for me. It may be different for you. Either way, to stop and stay stopped is a daily fight that gets easier with time.

Supplements

Let's look at some possible supplements you can consider to help with these withdrawal symptoms. St. John's Wort, Kava, 5-HTP, and a good B-complex. Let's look at each one individually. As always, consult with your doctor before taking these supplements!

St. John's Wort

Saint John's Wort is an herb. Mostly it is used for depression and it will help elevate your mood and eliminate some of the jitters and stress associated with the withdrawals. Weird imagery comes along with a name like Saint John's Wort, but fortunately it's available in capsule form. Another herb that falls into this category is Valerian root. It has similar properties and may also help with mucus build up when you're sick or your lungs are clearing up.

Kava Kava

Kava Kava is another herb that can help you relax and reduce anxiety. Try taking this as a tea in the evening. You have to drink it hot and sip it... hand to mouth... mimics something else...?

5-HTP

5-HTP stands for 5-hydroxy-tryptophan. It is a neurotransmitter that increases your natural production of serotonin. It is also being used for depression and weight loss. Tryptophan, an amino acid, can also be found naturally in foods like turkey, brown rice, cottage cheese, salmon, peanuts and soy protein.

As far as increasing natural release of serotonin, make sure you're getting enough B-6, vitamin-C, folate, and magnesium.

Most of what I'm talking about here can be found at your local health food store.

L-Theanine

Theanine is another amino acid that has a calming effect. It helps the body reduce levels of certain stress hormones. Namely, Cortisol and Epinephrine. It also can improve attentiveness and mental and physical function while reducing anxiety and promoting relaxation. It's also been known to be used in the treatment of ADD. Now I don't know about you, but this sounds like a nice natural complement to help ease the withdrawal. Green Tea has high contents of Theanine.

Vitamin-B

B-complex is necessary for normal brain function and since your brain has been rewired and is trying to handle life without nicotine and return to its original set up, it would aid in having a little help in the matter, so get on the B-complex at least.

The Stop Smoking Diet

Here's an example of daily eating that will flood your body with healthy energy.

Breakfast
1 cup 2% Greek Yogurt mixed with 1 cup frozen berries
16 oz. Water
Multi-Vitamin

Mid-Day Snack
Apple or Pear
16 oz. Water

Lunch
Grilled Chicken Caesar Salad or Greek Salad with Chicken
16 oz. Water
Multi-Vitamin

Afternoon Snack
A couple handfuls of Almonds
16 oz. Water

Dinner
Grilled Salmon
Asparagus, Spinach or Broccoli
Small Salad with Balsamic Vinaigrette
16 oz Water
Multi-Vitamin

<u>Desert</u>
A little bit of Dark Chocolate or Acai Berry Sorbet

Post-Exercise Meals

If you exercised well and you're within 2 hours of training and would like to eat some whole wheat pasta or brown rice, do so and enjoy. Otherwise, make it a point to avoid a lot of starch. High Fiber Carbs are OK (think beans)

A general guide line here would be to focus on eating foods that exist in nature and could be made or processed 2000 years ago. Just go WAY easy on the breads and avoid most things white. White rice, white breads, white sugar… all bad.

Day 2

Breakfast
3 eggs
Hamburger Patty
Cottage Cheese
8 oz Fresh Grapefruit Juice
Multi-Vitamin
16 oz Water

Snack
Peach or Plum
Handful of Almonds
16 oz Water

Lunch
Chicken and Steak Fajitas
No Rice or Tortilla
Whole Black Beans
Guacamole
Iced Tea with Lemon
Multi-Vitamin
16 oz Water

Snack
Apple or Fresh Berries
16 oz Water

Dinner
Grilled Chicken

Roasted Eggplant and Zucchini
Tossed Salad with Balsamic Vinaigrette
Multi-Vitamin
16 oz Water

<u>Desert</u>
Greek Yogurt with Crushed Pralines and Honey

See, it's not all that bad! What we're focusing on here is getting back to nature and reconnecting with our natural evolutionary metabolism. You may be one of those people who wind up losing weight instead of gaining weight.

Day 3

Breakfast
Smoothie made with Kefir, Blueberries, Raspberries, Strawberries and Banana
Multi-Vitamin

Snack
Small Can of Tuna and Celery
16 oz Water

Lunch
Chicken Kabobs
Persian Salad (chopped parsley, cucumbers and tomatoes in lemon juice)
Multi-Vitamin
16 oz Water

Snack
Beef Jerky
16 oz Water

Dinner
Cubed Chicken Breast tossed with Cut Asparagus and Cubed Eggplant woked in a light Teriyaki Sauce
Sliced Cucumbers with rice vinegar and sesame seeds
Multi-Vitamin
16 oz Water

Desert
Acai Berry Sorbet

Hopefully by now you can see a pattern forming and start getting an idea of what's possible and know you have many choices. Simply put, you know what's good for you. You just need to give yourself permission to act on it.

STEP 6-COMMITMENT: A 30 DAY CHALLENGE.

"The moment one definitely commits oneself, then providence moves too. All sorts of things occur to help one that would never have otherwise occurred… unforeseen incidents, meetings, and material assistance, which no man could have dreamed would have come his way."
-Gothe by way of Dyer

"Getterdun"

And now for the nitty-gritty. You as a smoking smoker, now have the arduous task of deciding to stop smoking (but don't quit). You're going to have to fool yourself just a little bit.

Remember in the first chapter I said to stop trying to quit because it's impossible? Then there's that joke, "I quit smoking every time I put one out! Then I start up again!" Stop me if you've heard this one before!

But here's the nitty-gritty, the real deal.

DECIDE not to smoke.

That's it?
YES!

DECIDE not to smoke.

The key now is to decide not to smoke.

Why not?!?! You *decided* to *start* smoking. You *decide* to smoke every time you light up. The key now is to decide *not* to smoke RIGHT NOW!

Let us not worry about a week from now or three hours from now. Let us only focus on *this* moment right now and in this moment make a conscious decision TO NOT HAVE A CIGARETTE!

Are You Kidding Me?

Are you getting pissed off because this sounds too simple and could never possibly work? I found out that because it is so simple, that it is the ONLY thing that will ever *really* work.

Sorry kids, there is no magic pill, patch, or gum or vapor that will cause you to quit. It is hard work and it is not only the decision to not smoke but the hard work that will save you.

Everything else is fluff. Period.

NOW

It is time to stop living in the past and dreaming about the future. You must decide to create your future NOW by living in this moment that you have now, because it is literally all you have. Stay in this moment and enjoy it for what it is. Worry about the next moment when you get there.

Ironically, you'll never arrive because it is always right now!

PRACTICE RUN

So let's try a little exercise. Take out a cigarette and put it in your mouth. Get your lighter out too.

Now instead of lighting it, put it back in the pack and say to yourself:

"For this moment, I choose not to smoke. I will deal with the next moment when it gets here."

Now repeat this statement whenever a craving hits and tuff it out! Write it down on an index card and carry it everywhere you go.

In the beginning it will be sheer agony and you may feel a little repetitive but stay at it. Keep yourself busy and commit to the moment. At first it will be a minute-by-minute battle. It may even be a second-by-second battle.

The good news is that within 24 hours it will be an hour-to-hour struggle and within a week, it'll be day-by-day.

MISSION POSSIBLE

Your mission should you choose to accept it, will be to not smoke *right now*. Continue on that path for the remainder of your life. If you choose to smoke again, that is your decision. Just remember, it is a decision you make and it is your decision, nobody else's. When you come to these moments in life, the real question is:

Are you going to hold on to a self-destructive behavior/habit for the sake of [fill in the black] or are you going to commit to the difficult challenge of transforming your life into something better?

Choice

The other thing you want to recognize is that between stimulation (craving) and response (smoking) there is a space. A moment where a decision is made and this applies to everything you do in life. This is your human essence and the foundation of your soul. It is the ability to select a response that makes us human and separates us from the animals that live strictly on instinct. You can see yourself in third person and be like Hamlet. *"To be or not to be, that is the question!"* To smoke or not to smoke, that is the question. What will you do? How do you want to live out the rest of your days? You will make that decision every moment, every day, every week, and every year for the rest of your life... no pressure though. How do you want to live out the rest of *your* life?

A quick story

Here's a quick story I'd like to impart on you. When I attended my first Kettlebell Certification Workshop, we were being instructed on a very intense workout that is designed to increase your aerobic work capacity and it is, as mentioned, very intense. It involves performing a snatch with the Kettlebell, basically, getting it overhead in one complete movement with one hand for repetitions for fifteen seconds. Then you get a fifteen second breather and then repeat with the other hand. Twenty minutes later, you can stop. It's an amazing routine and it requires a lot of intestinal fortitude. So, as we were being briefed on timing, form, and breathing, the Instructor,

Mark Reifkind, gave us a piece of wisdom to keep in our heads when we wanted to stop, give up or felt uncomfortable. It is a wisdom that you can apply to your quest of deciding not to smoke. Actually, I think this wisdom has multiple applications. Quite frankly, I wish I had heard this back in 2002. It actually might have made the process of stopping even easier for me. Hopefully, it will do the same for you. Here's what he said and it came from a Yoga instructor named Bikram Choudry the founder of Bikram Yoga,

"The pose does not begin, until you want to get out of it."

Isn't that perfect? What is your pose?

Getterdun, that's right!

So here it is. A challenge to decide not to smoke. And here's the kicker, I say decide to not smoke for a 30 day "trial period." If after 30 days of not smoking and learning to love yourself a little better you decide to start smoking again, do it. Yes, do it. You can, because you chose to stop and if you want to start back up, why not? Go for it. You won't, but you can, and therein lies the beauty. Why 30 days? Because 30 days is habit time, baby. Right? It takes 30 days to start a habit. Your new habit is *not* smoking! Try it. Do it! Commit to it for 30 days. That's all I'm asking. If you decide to make it a lifelong commitment, congratulations!

The good news is I'm going to walk you through the first 3 days…

Day 1

So this is day 1 of not smoking. How did you get here? Truthfully, it doesn't really matter all that much. What matters is that you're here now and you've made a decision. So, congratulations. One of the interesting things about this, and I'm sure I'm not the only one who's stopped like this, but sometimes stopping should be kind of an accident. You know what I mean? If you spend too much time preparing for it, thinking about it, eventually, it will become too big to handle. So today, do a few things to set yourself up for success. First and foremost, stay in the now. Don't spend any time on tomorrow or yesterday. Spend every waking moment in that moment. When the desire to smoke renders its ugly head, acknowledge it and say to yourself,

"This is another moment where I have the power to decide to smoke or not to smoke and for this moment, I decide to not smoke."

If you become anxious or agitated say,

"I have chosen to stop smoking, these sensations are my body returning to its natural state of being and they will pass."

What about other people? To your friends and family that you encounter throughout the day, the best thing to do is to have fun with them and with your challenge. So when you encounter them, simply apologize for yourself and the potentially sour-you that they may encounter over the next week or so. Now instantly get back into the moment of now.

You may be wondering why I'm suggesting only telling people you encounter about the journey you've undertaken and I'll tell you a story…

I had a buddy who tried to quit smoking like once a month. He'd tell everybody he was quitting and then would make it a day or two and then crack. He was like the boy who cried wolf and nobody took him seriously and he looked like a dork. Don't be that guy. Yes, get support! Yes, apologize for acting out on your withdrawal symptoms. When I stopped, I had a dry socket and was waiting tables and you know what? I made a bunch of money that week because every time I greeted a table I said, "Hello and welcome, my name's Dave, I'll be your waiter. I should also let you know that I had a wisdom tooth pulled that resulted in a dry socket and I haven't had a cigarette in 3 days so if I'm a bit punchy, I'd like to apologize in advance. However, your food and drinks will arrive in a timely manner. I simply cannot guarantee the friendly part. Now, would you care to start off with a cocktail or an appetizer?" Everyone laughed and tipped well.

It is your good attitude that will get you through day 1 and beyond.

Day 2

Look familiar? Yeah. 24 hours without a smoke. I'm sure you've done this before, right? They say the first three days are the hardest. I say day two is the hardest because you've been here before. Now what? Keep deciding not to smoke, that's what! 24 hours down and 48 more to go and then you're home free!

Yesterday you were probably in a minute-to-minute struggle with your subconscious. Today may be the same; however, see if you can extend the gaps between re-deciding not to smoke. See if you can take it out from the minute-by-minute decision process to hour-by-hour. Say to yourself,

"SELF, I made it that last hour. Let's do one more hour and take it from there!"

Then repeat that for the next 24 – 48 hours.

Also, yesterday was kind of a let's just get through it day. You know what I mean? Now today is where the real work begins. Make YOUR BREATHING your key focus today. Not simply because you're going to be breathing better as your body goes back to its natural smoke free state, but also your body may be a little confused on what that natural state may be. Your body might be under the impression that nicotine delivered through the inhalation of tobacco smoke *is* its natural state and might start feeling a little anxious about changing things up a bit.

How do you deal with the feeling of anxiety? Breathe. Deep breathing to be exact! We're going to go at this one Karate Kid style. As Mr. Miyagi said, "In through nose, out through mouth." Breathe slowly and deliberately. Make sure to keep your back straight. You can do it sitting, standing or lying down. Do it once, do it twice. Do it for 10 minutes. However long it takes.

As you inhale, bring with it good thoughts and energy. As you exhale, release negativity and anxiety. You can do this throughout the day and for the rest of your life actually whenever negative energy tries to take a grip on you.

This is also a primary step into quieting the mind. Not that my mind is quiet. Oh God no! However, taking a moment or two out of your day to focus on your breathing and energy is an excellent tool for dealing with your primary cause of stress which right now is not smoking. Later on as you recognize that smoking relieved a lot of stress and you're stressed out and since you've decided not to smoke today what are you going to do…? Yup! You guessed it! BREATHE!

So for today, focus on not smoking this hour, in the now. Deal with the next hour when you get there.

In the in-between times, deep breathing to relax.

You should be very proud of yourself as you complete day two.

Now, just get through tomorrow and you're on the non-smoking superhighway.

Day 3

Congratulations! You're on day three! You just went 48 hours without a cigarette! You know what this means right? It means that if you made it these last two days, then the only reason, the only thing keeping you from continuing on, is you.

Think about that for a second. You have this amazing power to choose your actions. Now you just continue to not smoke. Yes it is that simple and yes it is effing hard. Get over it!

Today continue going with hour by hour re-commitments to not smoke. Take the little victory of not smoking each hour and use it build momentum.

I read a book called *"Sales Dogs"* by Blair Singer, and in it, he's talking to salespeople about a few key and basic tools and principles for a sales person's mind set. One of those little tools, which can convert into a big tool and make a profound change on your attitude, is to "Celebrate All Wins." Every hour you go without a smoke is a win. Take a quick private moment to yourself, make a fist with your right hand, pull it in toward your side and say something like,

"Yes!" or "That's right, nicotine, you got nothing on me! Another hour without you! What do you got? Nothing! That's what!"

Yes, trash talkin' to your addiction is an effective tool for not smoking. There is the potential for embarrassment if you get too into it, but who cares really! You're not smoking and you're having fun with it.

Celebrate the life you're giving yourself and the confidence you're manually imputing into your daily life. You're making a major accomplishment and you should be proud of yourself. This is hard work and you deserve to praise yourself not only for deciding to stop but to stay stopped.

You also want to take some time to express gratitude today and for everyday hereafter. This road your on will be a hard road and it requires inner strength that you have already and are now using to accomplish this task. Earlier I talked about working for a purpose greater than yourself. You don't have to believe in God, but this is a good time to just be grateful for all the tools you naturally have to achieve this task.

Today is also a good day to start looking ahead a little bit. Wait! What?

Why? Hold on! Wait a second now! I thought we were staying "in the now?" We are, but I want you to think about and visualize a year from now. It's been almost three days without a smoke. You can do this. You've done it and you are doing it right now. You can continue to do it a year from now. So you might as well start acting as if *that* now (of being a year without smoking) is already here. Let me hear you say it loud and proud.

"I am so very proud of myself and so very grateful that it is one year from now and I've decided to not smoke this whole year. I think I'll do that for another year!"

Day four's gonna be a walk in the park for you!

STEP 7-LIBERATION.

"Between stimulus and response there is a space. In that space is our power to choose our response. In our response lies our growth and our freedom."
-Viktor Frankl

Crossroads

When at any crossroads in life, always go to the gangster film for advice. I have found many a good piece of advice in the gangster movie. Lots of life lessons in the gangster movie!

At these particular crossroads, I shall refer you to the *Untouchables* with Sean Connery. He asks Kevin Costner, "What are you prepared to do?" I ask of you, what are *you* prepared to do? What are you prepared to give? My teenage idol, Humphrey Bogart died from cancer of the esophagus at age 58. I'm sorry, but I am NOT checking out at 58. I want grandkids on my knee. I want to enjoy my old age and not suffer like that. Even if I do die of cancer and suffer, I want to go down knowing I stopped killing myself. What do you think Bogie was thinking as he lay there, "Well schwee-hart, instead of the Camel, maybe I should have just walked the mile…?"

Well, not *me* baby! To hell with that! I ain't going out like that. What about you? What do you want out of life and what are you prepared to do in order to reach your goals? How are you earning your future?

A little exercise for you:

In your journal, write about your future.

- What are your dreams?
- Can you turn them into goals?
- Can you write your future?

Current Situations

Since stopping smoking, I feel like I have returned to the real me. Smoking isn't part of the "real" me and it isn't the "real" you either. Ironically, I had to smoke to find that out. I have a wife now and I am looking forward to growing old with her and making babies. Everything seems possible now.

Do I miss it? Hell yes! Will I go back? Nope! Never! Not gonna happen. I'm too busy in the now and the future to go back. Why would I? The mere idea of having to stop all over again is motivation enough to not start up again. Every once in a blue moon, I'll have a cigar. I'll enjoy it for what it is, in that moment and smoke Bill Clinton style, meaning I don't inhale. The romance comes back and I'm "cool" again. Then for the next 24 hours after my fingers smell like I've given a cow a proctology exam, my tongue tastes like an ashtray and

I'm reminded of all the reasons why I stopped doing this in the first place.

When I see other people smoke now, I think back to not being able to run like I can now or snatch a kettlebell over my head 100 times in 5 minutes. I think about being short of breath, about the smell of my car and having to excuse myself from either family interaction or time with my girlfriend, now wife, to go smoke.

Time is so precious, so valuable, so dear, and once you spend it, it doesn't come back. Spend it wisely.

For me, I have come around full circle. I started smoking out of rebellion. Still, I am a rebel. I started to lose interest in smoking when I realized I couldn't function without cigarettes. My whole life revolved around my next cigarette and eventually, that pissed me off. I don't like being that out of control. Big Tobacco's got a hold on me brother! I had to rebel against that system. I bought what they were selling. I fell for it hook, line and filter. Lights? Light cigarettes? Come on, who are we kidding? Ourselves! Filter, non-filter, who cares, you're inhaling over 4,000 chemicals, 43 of which are known to cause cancer. There is no such thing as light cancer.

"What kind of cancer do you have, Bob?"

"Oh, me, I have the light cancer!"

Give me a break! Stop fooling yourself and letting these people profit from your misery and self-medicating.

When I look at the big picture, I see a lot of powerful people in society that attempt to convince us all that we are not in control of our lives. That when you do something wrong it isn't your fault. You were abused as a child so you're excused from the abuse you perpetrate on others. Your father cheated on your mother, so it's normal or understandable that you too would cheat on your wife. Reality TV is rewarding and glamorizing inappropriate behavior. You have these rappers out there teaching kids it's OK to be a "gangsta." That to make it you have to be a drug dealer or a killer first. What ever happened to hard work? Bill Clinton, a fine role model and his wife, the pillar of moral fortitude. Let me tell you something, he broke a promise he made to God. You *don't* do that. And as a wife, she stays with him? I thought she was a feminist? What was learned America? What is being learned and taught to our kids? What are you teaching your kids if you smoke? Do as I say not as I do? I had relatives that would tell me not to smoke. I'd get whole dissertations on how I shouldn't fall into the smoking trap with a "can you pass the ashtray" injected in there for effective irony. Come on people!!! It's OK to do something wrong, as long as you're really sorry after the fact??? How does that work?

What does this have to do with smoking? Nothing really. What does it have to do with choice? Everything. And that has everything to do with smoking.

Do not let society or anyone try to convince you that you are not in control. You are in control of every single second of your life. Your behavior is your own regardless of your past and only you right now in this moment can decide the next moment.

Another little story

I remember working at this restaurant, and every afternoon this guy in his 50's would come in with his business partner and the two of them would sit on the patio and drink 2 glasses of house chardonnay and smoke 7 cigarettes *each* in about an hour and a half. I remember this guy's face looked like a saddle. Yes, the thing you sit on, when you ride a horse. His fingers were yellowish and he looked like he was 70. Not 50. His voice was raspy, like he had a bad cold all the time. You could hear the mucus in his lungs. His walk was labored; he was skinny in an unhealthy kind of skinny way. He was dying. Right before my eyes this poor bastard was slowly killing himself and this woman he was with smoked right along with him as if it wasn't real and didn't apply to them, cancer and emphysema are for the other smokers, not us. She looked just like him. I'm grateful to have known them because they helped me stay stopped.

I'm selfish in that I love my wife and family too much to want to leave the party too soon. Besides, it's rude to leave too early! When you're at a good party, you never want to leave early. You might miss something. I'm going to stay at this party called life until God comes and kicks my ass out.

I also have given myself permission to be loved and realize that other people love me too and don't want me to leave the party too soon either. My wife is the life of my party and I am the life of her party. How could I leave early? If it's time, it's time, if the choir's singing and Bob Dylan's talking about mama taking this badge off of me, then let's go, but I'm not going to do anything as self-destructive as smoking 20 plus cigarettes a day to speed things up. I have way too much to live for.

How about YOU?

What do you live for? Aside from nicotine, what do you live for? **Because that was your answer!**

If you're smoking now, that *was* your response. Yes, it was. Stop lying to yourself and admit you're addicted and need to stop. If not for your sake, for the sake of those who love you. So, figure out what you live for. Know that you are loved. Know you are not alone. Live a long life. Decide to live that long life. Stop smoking and stop trying to kill yourself. You deserve much better. Even if you don't believe it, keep saying it until you do.

If nobody loves you, if that was your gut instinctual response right there, it's bullshit. Somebody loves you but you haven't given them permission or yourself permission to be loved. So, maybe you've done some rotten stuff. Well, then fix it. Fix it dear Henry, dear Henry, dear Henry, fix it.

(Please excuse the non-sequitur Sesame Street reference)

Now, reach out! And if you've done some really rotten stuff, just move on. Let's say you're 52, living alone in an old apartment downtown, you're on disability, you're wife and kids abandoned you because you were abusive and you spend your days reading crime novels, watching old reruns on TV and drinking generic whiskey and smoking GPCs. Your face is older than you should be and you feel sorry for yourself constantly. Sounds kind of romantic doesn't it? The old rat bastard sitting there waiting for his son to come home and save him.

Screw that! Save yourself, start over, it's never too late to…

- First, stop being a rat bastard,
- Second, stop smoking, and
- Finally start LIVING again.

Go make new friends, get another wife, move forward. Move into the now and the future. There's nothing for you back there. I promise. Go make new friends, get another wife, move forward. Yes I did mean to put that down twice. Look, you're moving forward either way, the question is, how would you like to move forward?

Ah… it's too late!

No, it's not! It's never too late to reclaim the rest of your life!

"We can stop, but it will not be through the good intention or resolutions… we will stop when we grow truly desperate and then truly committed – when some force or source of inspiration bigger than our ego takes command, and our Basic Self surrenders to a higher will."

-Dan Millman

Choice, Purpose and a Paradox

Each and every one of us does have something to live for. It is at this point that I would like to toss in a little paradoxical thinking for those of you struggling with having something to live for. This next idea will seem paradoxical to westerners and should make perfect since to our friends who are well versed in Eastern Philosophy.

It is after all this talk of choice that I would like to propose that you seriously consider the following.

Even if you don't know your purpose or believe that you personally have nothing to live for, I guarantee that you do and challenge you to put some faith in a higher power and know that this higher power does have a plan for you and that everything *is* being orchestrated to some degree *and* everything so far and from this moment on will have purpose, meaning and happen right on time according to plan.

Whose plan? Who cares *whose* plan it is! That's for you atheists and agnostics out there to figure out. I never mentioned "God" in there. I'm not talking about the grey haired guy who made us in his image or any of that. Earlier, I mentioned Star Wars. Think of this "Power" I'm referring to as the Force.

"It's an energy field created by all living beings. It surrounds us, penetrates us and binds the galaxy together."

There's a lot of wisdom in those movies! It's real. Trust me. Heck, trust yourself; you know deep down it's there. You've already had too many coincidences to not believe in a high power.

Does this Force have a consciousness? *I* think so. However, that one is up to you, but I want you to at least believe in a greater purpose and a purpose greater than you and allow yourself to decide to be guided by that Force or purpose.

How did you and I meet?

Look at me, I'm the guy writing this and you're reading it. Cosmically, we were meant to meet like this. In the same vein, you have purpose and there is a plan for you. You don't have to know exactly what it is, just be open to it and allow yourself to be guided a little bit in the same way you stumbled upon this little piece of literature (yeah right, literature...)

The Trolley Strap

A very wise man, Wayne Dyer, refers to this as "grabbing the trolley strap." Think about being on a trolley or subway. Life is the trolley, God or the Force is driving, whichever is easier for you to accept right now, you choose to get on board (remember the thing on choice and the paradox of purpose). Now when this baby gets moving, you don't want to fall or stumble, so you grab that strap that hangs there and now you can enjoy the ride.

Rental Car Return

In AA they say "let go and let God." If you decide to be open to it, you will find your purpose and it might be safe to say that everything that has happened in your life up to now has happened so you can learn and grow into the perfect creation that you are now and you can celebrate by deciding to nurture this physical manifestation of the Force that is your body instead of treating it like a trash can. Look at your life like renting a car. You got to give it back the way you got it. Now some people dog their rental cars. You need to love this rental and definitely make sure it goes back in good condition.

CONCLUSION

The Next Steps

For now, that's it. Feel free to be a smoker and decide not to smoke. It's your decision to make and if this has helped great. If not, stop smoking anyway!

So now what? You're there, you're thinking to yourself,

"I can do this! I can stop! I have the power to do it!"

The time to stop is yesterday. It's now. How you do it is up to you. If you're in the now, now, and NOT smoking as you read this, then you've already stopped. Get it? You staying this way is totally on you. You decided to start. Decide to stop.

Here's my story until now.

In May of 2002, I had a wisdom tooth removed. It had popped up and it was quite infected. Not very comfortable to say the least. In fact the pain was quite severe. I didn't have insurance or much money either and knew I needed a dentist. Insurance and waiters don't mix well.

It's rather funny how the people handling your food are not provided with insurance by the company unless they work over 35 hours a week and the management schedules you 33.5 hours a week. Then when you actually need to call in sick, they tell you to get a doctor's note… but I'm not bitter.

The point being is I had to cover the bill on my own and was broke. I had to shop around for a best price exam. I found a guy that agreed to apply the price of the exam to the work should I choose his service, which I did. He offered to remove the tooth right away with a local anesthesia. Being that I hadn't been to a dentist in years, I was a little scared… ok, how about terrified by the fact that in under ten minutes this "nice man" would be working on my mouth like the Spanish Inquisition. I mean, we just met. Never mind the 24 inch hypodermic needle he just pulled out... I mean, are you going to buy me a few drinks first? Will we cuddle afterwards? Breakfast? Will you even still be there in the morning?

I felt I needed a day to sort this out. Also, I kinda wanted my mommy, but that's beside the point.

I decided to treat myself and opted for the general anesthesia. I felt I needed to be out cold. So somewhere in the confusion of it all after it was all done, I was driven home by my girlfriend, I hobbled up to my apartment, high as a kite, plopped down on the patio and had myself a cigarette. What's nicer than a smoke when you're numb and loaded? To this day, I don't remember being told anything about "no sucking" in the first 24 hours. Apparently, it was made perfectly clear but I don't remember because I was HIGH! Nitrous, Vicodin, and whatever else they pumped into me floundered my good senses a tad...

Either way, I wound up with a dry socket. What are you gonna do?

For those of you not familiar with the term, "dry socket" is a condition in which the blood clot from the extraction site is lost and it leaves BONE AND NERVE endings exposed to the elements of the mouth. Needless, to say it hurt more than having the tooth in there. If I thought the infection was painful, this was like ten times that. Really close to a kick in the nuts. Really close.

The dentist told me that in order for this to heal properly, I needed to not smoke for three to five days and come in daily to have this eucalyptus gel stuffed in my hole. The hole in my mouth that is. I know what you're thinking, what kind of sick dentist is this? But, I digress.

So there I was. At the crossroads. I thought, hell, I can go a couple of days and not smoke. I've been thinking about quitting anyway. This can be a nice trial run. I told myself, just get through the next three days and take it from there. I had every intention of continuing on smoking in three days. So it was on. I had one last cigarette on the way to my girlfriend's apartment and began the process. The first six hours were easy. As a waiter, I could go 6-8 hours without a cigarette. I got through it because it was so busy, I didn't have time to smoke.

But now this was different. I wasn't busy. In the morning, I drank my coffee in my right hand. My left hand, horribly, lonely. No big cravings yet. By mid-morning, I was getting pretty anxious. I hit the gym and ran. After my workout, I felt really good. I also really wanted a cigarette.

I then had my revelation. I remembered something from my acting classes. **Live moment to moment in the scene**. I thought if I can get through this moment now, I don't have to worry about the next moment, just stay in the NOW and I'll be OK. So, I stayed in the moment as best as I could.

I also dove into the science of nicotine. I kept myself as busy as possible and every time I had a craving, I told myself, "For this moment, I choose not to smoke! I will deal with the next moment when it gets here."

After a couple of days, my hole was feeling better. After the first day I was sitting on my patio with my roommate, who was still smoking, and right in front of me! Thanks a$$hat... Appreciate the support! It's alright, that's what addiction can do to people. Then, I realized something else. This sucks.

"Quitting" sucks.

This sucks! It's impossible to quit. I can't do this no matter how hard I try.

I am twelve inches away from a pack of cigarettes and the urge to light up is *almost* unbearable.

[**NOTE:** Almost being the key word here]

I wanted to jump off the balcony, climb the walls, my head felt as if it was to explode and I felt as if couldn't breathe. Inside I was screaming in agony.

I managed to keep reminding myself over and over again that in two more days, I can have a cigarette and that for right now I am just going to decide not to smoke.

By the end of three very monotonous days, I just could not justify smoking. I had just spent three days in dire agony and knew how far I had come. I had stopped!

I took it one day at a time and decided to continue taking it one day at a time. I also took it upon myself to apologize in advance to everyone I came into contact with for that first week. However, even still to this day, I refuse to admit that I have "quit." I can still smoke anytime I want. This carrot dangling technique has been most effective!

It's been years now since my last cigarette and I can say with full certainty I have no intention of ever having a cigarette again. However, who knows? The bottom line is I have the power to decide my next action and I am free from addiction because I choose to be.

APPENDIXES & AFTERTHOUGHTS

"I Can't do it"

"You're not dying, you just can't think of anything better to do!" -Ferris Bueller

There are examples of people who went through some *real* adversity so stop saying you can't. If these folks can live through this and smile again, you can stop smoking. So quit whining and start stopping smoking!

Ever feel like a book is too short? I do. I do now. I want to tell you more, yet I think I'm done spouting. However, I do think some other people have some valuable lessons for you. Especially in the face of some *real* adversity.

I'm going to list off a few people who survived worse experiences that you and me wrestling with nicotine addiction and not smoking anymore. This way you can have an even greater appreciation of your life, of how precious it is, and I want you to want to make it a little longer. I look to these people for inspiration and motivation…

-**When lacking willpower**, look to Ghandi and Viktor Frankle. Both these men are a testament to true conviction.

-**When you need strength**, look to Dan Millman. A true peaceful warrior who knows how to live in the now.

-**When faith is required**, see Mother Theresa and Saint Francis of Assisi.

-**For wisdom**, seek Wayne Dyer and Yoda.

-**If you need a good shot of "in your face**," turn your radio dial to Dr Laura. (You don't have to agree with her views, but do try to feel and capture some of her resolve)

The Smoker's Workout

Learning to use your lungs again!

Get some comfortable shoes on and find a hill. It doesn't have to be a big hill but it definitely can't be a small little pitcher's mound of a hill either. Just find a nice decent little hill. It can have grass, like a park or if you're in the city, a hill with a sidewalk. If there are no hills, find some stairs or a treadmill that inclines just don't find me an excuse, OK?

So now walk up that hill! Get to the top. How was that? Are you winded? Good. Now walk back down. Do you have your breath back? Excellent! Walk back up! I know you were just up there, but do it again…

Here's your schedule.

4 days a week, you pick the days and time. BUT, First thing in the morning is best though, if you want my opinion. Get it done and out of the way.

Week 1:
Day 1 – Walk up 4 times.
Day 2 – Walk up 4 times.

Day 3 – Walk up 5 times.
Day 4 – Walk up 5 times.

Week 2:
Day 1 – Walk up 4 times.
Day 2 – Walk up 5 times.
Day 3 – Walk up 6 times.
Day 4 – Walk up 6 times.

Week 3:
Day 1 – Walk up 5 times.
Day 2 – Walk up 6 times.
Day 3 – Walk up 7 times.
Day 4 – Walk up 7 times.

See the pattern? Get to 10 times and then start over, but now you're going to walk faster up that hill. Not a run yet, not even a jog, just walk as if you're late for something. When you're at 10 on the brisk hill walk, now try the jog.

Work up to running. You can do it if you commit. Come on, you committed to smoking, now commit to you and your body!

If there comes a day where motivation is low and lacking, I highly suggest adding the soundtrack to Rocky to your musical library as it is perfect for getting pumped up for exercise even when you're nowhere near the mood for exercise. So what if it's cheesy. That's why God invented headphones. No one has to know…

Evening strength training!

So if you've been doing this walk/jog routine for a while and you're doing it in the morning, what's the next step? Evening strength training! Three times a week and let's keep it super simple. How many pushups can you do? What about Sit Ups? Deep Knee Bends? Let's make some notes.

I can do ____ Pushups.
I can do ____ Sit Ups.
I can do ____ Deep Knee Bends.

Was the answer 0 across the board? Let's assume it was for now.

What about pushups on your knees?

I can do ____ pushups from my knees.

For the Pushups, get in the pushup position, as if you're about to do a push up and hold it for as long as you can.

I can hold a push up position for ____ seconds.

If you can't do a sit up yet, how much of a sit up can you do? If you can't do a deep knee bend or a squat, just sit in a chair and stand back up.

Your goal is 25 of each. Start small and build up over time just like the walking. If you're already at the 25 of each, make it 50, 75, 100! Just get to work!

When you decide to make the commitment to a stronger body; a lot more than just your body winds up getting strong. I promise you that.

For a great selection of exercise books for any fitness level, visit:
http://www.stopdontquit.com/store.html

Understanding a bit about EGO

Initially, I had no intention on touching on this thing called ego, but after reviewing what I had written, I changed my mind. Let's start with what ego is.

The word "ego" is Latin for "I". Webster's Dictionary says Ego is a noun and it has three possible meanings. *1. An inflated feeling of pride in your own superiority to others. 2. Your consciousness of your own identity. 3. (psychoanalysis) the conscious mind.*

Our good buddy Sigmund Freud would tell you that ego stands in between the Id and the Superego to balance our primitive needs and our moral/ethical beliefs… Uh… yeah, whatever dude…

The best definition I've found and the one we're going to go with for this book comes from Wayne Dyer's book, "The Power of Intention."

"We humans, however, with our capability for presumably higher brain functions, have something we refer to as ego, which is an idea that we construct about who and what we are."

Feel free to read that as many times as necessary for that to really sink in. Pay special attention to the *"idea that we construct about who and what we are"* part.

Once you have a handle on the fact that your idea of who you are is something you create, you can then tackle the idea that who you think you are may not necessarily actually be *who* you really are. Get it?

Your ego will separate you from you. This can help you or hurt you. Once you realize you're not your possessions or what others think of you, you're free to really be you, but if you believe you are your work, your bank account, your car and that you have to live up to what you think others think of you, your separated from the real you, your real self and from any real living.

What's the point? The point is this: you don't have to identify with anything to be you. I'm a smoker. I know that and I am that. I've accepted it and choose to not smoke. I do that because I'm not separate from my body or anything else for that matter.

Yeah, my ego kicks in sometimes, but who's doesn't? However, I have gained enough control over it to accept and invite my connection to God, The Force, The Power of Intention, other beings and any type of energy I encounter is this mysterious universe.

Like I said earlier, I didn't have to smoke to be cool. I smoked because I am cool and now that I've chosen not to smoke; do you know what I found out? Holy smoke, I'm still cool! Don't you want to be cool too? C'mon, everybody's doing it…

See what I did there?

The go it alone approach? For God's sake get some help!

So what's the bottom line? Make sure you have a support network. If all your friends smoke, maybe it's time for new friends or at least a break until you're back in control of your actions. They'll understand. If not, screw 'em, because they're not really your friends. You don't have to go it alone, that's the point.

My Two Cents On Chantix

OK, let me fire off a quick disclaimer and then I'll get into my opinion.

Not smoking anymore is the goal. A few pages back, I tell you plainly, "For God's sake, get some help!" If it's a prescription medication that gets you there, so be it. Not necessary if you ask me, but if that's what you need, that's what you need.

That's the disclaimer. Now for the nitty, the gritty, one dose of however and a big but (pun intended).

If you just wind up replacing one addiction for another, why bother? That's the point. Consider methadone for a moment. How is that a good idea? So you're off heroin but hooked on methadone and when you try to get off the methadone, you're back on the heroin. Vicious cycle.

So out on the market is Chantix, a drug that is in a class of drugs for smoking cessation.

Wikipedia calls it a smoking cessation aid. Meaning it's there to help but not do the job. I'm OK with that part. Here's where I have a problem:

"Important Safety Information:

Some people have had changes in behavior, hostility, agitation, depressed mood, suicidal thoughts or actions while using Chantix to help them quit smoking. Some people had these symptoms when they began taking Chantix, and others developed them after several weeks of treatment or after stopping Chantix. If you, your family, or caregiver notice agitation, hostility, depression, or changes in behavior, thinking, or mood that are not typical for you, or you develop suicidal thoughts or actions, anxiety, panic, aggression, anger, mania, abnormal sensations, hallucinations, paranoia, or confusion, stop taking Chantix and call your doctor right away. Also tell your doctor about any history of depression or other mental health problems before taking Chantix, as these symptoms may worsen while taking Chantix."

Are you effing kidding me right now?!?! Is this some kind of joke or SNL sketch? Coming from someone who's been there and done that, what does a change in behavior with hostility, agitation, and depressed mood sound like to you? If you've ever gone 9 hours without a cigarette, you know exactly what that sounds like. WITHDRAWAL!!!

In addition, while taking this I may want to kill myself. From where I'm standing, I'm trying to quit smoking here people! I want to stop because I want to live! Now that I'm not smoking and I'm not speeding up the lung, prostate, throat, mouth cancer, heart disease, emphysema because I finally found a little extra love for myself and want to extend my life... (deep breath) So, why am holding a gun to my head?

Let's get one thing real straight here. When I went through withdrawals, I was hostile, agitated, depressed, anxious, panicky, overly aggressive, angry, and manic. I had violent and suicidal thoughts, abnormal sensations (like breathing better) mild hallucinations (I saw cigarettes everywhere!) and paranoia (not Naked Lunch style more like the first five minutes of Fear and Loathing in Las Vegas) and I was incredibly confused. So please, someone explain the value of this drug to me? From where I'm standing, if you go cold turkey, you're gonna get to put up with all this crap anyway?

So to add insult to injury, taking this medication might also result in a rash that can become life threatening. My face could swell up from an allergic reaction. So too my mouth and throat may swell in a way that may cut off my air supply. If I have these symptoms or a rash with peeling or blisters in my mouth, I'm supposed to stop taking it and call my doctor right away.

Really? Well that's some sound advice!

Personally, I'll take the ashtray breath and periodontal disease over this crap. But wait, it gets better! Apparently, the most common side effects are nausea, sleep problems, constipation, gas and or vomiting.

CO-WORKER 1: "Hi Bob! How are you today?"

BOB: "Well, Cheryl, I'm pretty pissed off for no good reason and this hostility just seems to keep bubbling up inside of me. I'm getting more and more depressed and can't seem to shake this anxiety. So much so that I'm thinking about jumping off the roof after I finish those reports for Sam I Am who keeps looking over my shoulder telling me that it's OK my spleen is vibrating, which I think is somehow directly related to the Kennedy assassination, and I'm not talking about Jack or Bobby. You gotta know Ed was whacked! But listen Julie, I'm glad you asked me how I was feeling because I think I'm getting a rash on my tongue, but can't seem to see it because I'm so nauseous I'm afraid to open my mouth because I don't want to throw up again. I'm starting to swell and I'm not sure if the bloating is a reaction or just gas. You know, the Russians are putting something in the water that will only allow you to have a bowel movement every third Saturday of the month? I learned that from a dream I had and you know it was Woody Woodpecker who figured it out and trusted me with the data. But hey! I haven't had a cigarette in 6 days! I think I'm gonna go down stairs and take that forklift for a test drive!"

What?

Look kids, it's like this. In a nut shell, and if I've said it once, I'll say it again, you can't quit. It's impossible to quit, so don't even try.

Quitting sucks. You're going to feel miserable in the beginning and great at the end. How do you like to take off a band-aid? Quick, right? Why prolong the agony? Don't trade one addiction for the other. If you have a chemical imbalance in your brain, go see a psychiatrist and get help. There's nothing to be ashamed of, but keep this in mind too. If you smoke or ingest nicotine, you're brain and body is physically addicted. That in itself is a chemical imbalance in your brain. Your body will have the capacity to repair itself and re-balance. However, sooner or later, you gotta suffer the pains of withdrawal. You chose to smoke and most likely are still smoking as a form of self-medication. When you step up and stop, you'll have to, as my buddy Charlie says, "Cowboy up" and as Larry the Cable Guy puts it, "getterdone." If you can get through it all on your own, you'll be better for it. Take it from someone who has!

That's the point. So today's lesson is simple, if you want to stop smoking, Cowboy up and getterdone!

By the way, if you'd like to do a cost/comparison analysis, a pack of 56 of these wonder pills will run you on average 135 bucks. The recommendation is 12 weeks. That's 3 months. $405 to get off smoking and be like Bob. This book, How to Stop Smoking Without Killing Anyone is a one-time minimal investment for a lifetime of success.

Dave, what's your take on NRT (Nicotine Replacement Therapy)?

Stupid. Do or do not, there is no try.

"What is the most effective way right now for patients who really want to stop smoking?"

This was the question asked to Dr. John Hallberg from Tom Crann of All Things Considered on NPR.

Let's look at Hallberg's answer.

HALLBERG: I wish there was "the way" -- that there was a single way to make this happen. I think that over and over again, the thing that comes up is the importance of setting a quit date; that looking out ahead, something significant on the calendar that becomes the date that that person kind of wraps their mind around that they will quit. And then starting to decrease the nicotine and getting up to that point, considering using a nicotine replacement substance when the time comes, such as a patch or a spray or an inhaler, possibly medication. But there is no single way, I'm afraid.

My two cents on the matter... here we go...

WEAK ANSWER!

C'mon Dr. Hallberg! People look to you for more than advice. They look to you for strength and motivation. Give it to them and take a stand on something. Say it load and proud and mean it.

#1. There is a way to make this happen! The human brain is so powerful. We put a man on the moon and created this internet that I'm communicating with potentially millions of people. Cliché as it may be, where there is a will there is a way. The power of decision and choice is the most powerful human element If you can decide to start something then you can decide to stop something.

#2. Weaning off may not be the best solution. For some it has worked, but I know for me, it didn't. What worked was deciding to stop. When a person makes a real decision to stop smoking, they suddenly find the ability and strength to stop. Once a person fully, truly and sincerely commits to something the whole world will move to aid in the quest. If you're truly committed, you'll do it. Be responsible for your choices. Yes, smoking, even after it has become an addiction is still a choice. You are not helpless.

"You are powerful beyond measure." - Marianne Williamson

#3. Setting a date and making a big deal out of quitting only ads to the anxiety of the situation and for some just delays the taking of action.

Yoda-ism #1, "Do or do not. There is no try." Action is the final key. Smokers need to go beyond, "this is bad for me" if that was all it took, no one would smoke. We all know it's bad and we decide to do it anyway. That's insane. Period. If you're going to stop, you need to find a reason bigger than you, commit to that reason and then re-commit every time you feel the urge. That's all it is you know. It's just an urge. With the advent of caller-ID, how many times do you deny the urge to answer the phone? Just hit the ignore button when nicotine calls. Simple? Yes. Easy? HELL NO! Do it anyway...

"But there is no single way, I'm afraid."

He is afraid. Damn right. Chicken$hit! Afraid to speak the truth. That you, a human being, can stop. Addiction is powerful. But it's not all powerful.

Smokers and addicts alike, you're not helpless.

Here's the way - change a couple of mind sets here:

#1. The time to stop smoking was yesterday. Take action, decide to stop and commit to it. Commit to it for a purpose greater than you.

#2. Addiction is not a reason to keep smoking, it's an excuse to keep smoking. It's a powerless place to be. Take the power back. Every time you light up moving forward, acknowledge that you are choosing to smoke and that you can equally choose NOT to smoke.

#3. Every time you say "can't" replace it in your mind with "won't." I can't stop smoking! I won't stop smoking. Why won't you stop? Because I'm addicted to it! Remember #2, that's just an excuse. I'm choosing to smoke and I can choose to stop. I have the power to stop.

Leave quitting out of it. Quitting may be too big a concept for your addicted brain. For now, just stop; don't quit.

e-Cigarettes: What is the deal? (spoken in Seinfeld voice)

Searching e-cigarettes on Twitter will surely do one very specific thing. Confuse the crap out of you! Look at this, the Huffington Post says the vapor juice can increase your chances of getting a really hard to beat staph infection while Reuters says it's a great way to quit. Both of these should fall under the hashtag WTF.

Allow me to weigh in on this one. Forget all you think you know about the e-cigarette for a second and let's put some attention on traditional cigarettes; you know the one's with actual tobacco. Habitual and consistent smoking of tobacco cigarettes will lead to an early death. Period. Usually the early death comes with severe pain and suffering as well. Sure, someone's Grandmother smoked and lived to be 82 and her heart stopped one night while she slept.

Consider this. How long would she have gone if she hadn't smoked, first of all and secondly, YOU are not that woman. Those lucky few are exceptions to the rule and we seek them out to provide us comfort and to avoid the reality that continuing this habit will lead us to an early grave.

Contemplating our own mortality is never easy. We tend to create a mindset where we don't have to look it square in the eye. Look at the marketing done by cigarette companies from the get go. They were glamorous and showed people living. Celebrities endorsed them, movies used them, doctors and opera singers were paid to recommend certain brands, tobacco companies gave cigarettes to the troops during both world wars. Nothing about their advertising speaks of an early death wrought with pain and disease. Rather, tobacco companies put up images like the Marlboro Man and Virginia Slims show progressive women. They want you to feel ALIVE when you smoke, not setting yourself up for a bad exit. Following me so far?

Now, what is happening right now in the world of the electronic cigarette? They call it an e-cigarette. Makes it sound totally harmless. Like e-mail or e-commerce. And now, you don't smoke an e-cigarette, you vape. Because it's just vapor. Right? Harmless. Right? Sure... I guess. And that's the problem isn't it? We're guessing for now... just like 100 years ago. What else is similar? Celebrity endorsements? Freedom themed marketing? A healthy alternative?

At the end of the day, either way, you're rolling the dice. At the end of the day you still wind up addicted to nicotine. When the smoke settles (pun intended) you must recognize that every time you light up, electronic or otherwise you are handing over control of your mood, decisions, finances and life to a chemical that is lethal at 30-60 mg in humans, weakens the immune system, elevates blood pressure, messes with your hormones, all kinds of stuff, so while you're not dealing with the tar and smoke from tobacco, you're really just exchanging one set of complications from your addiction for another and yes, you're still addicted. The downside of addiction is for another conversation altogether, but nicotine is not good for you no matter how you chose to deliver it to yourself. And you deserve total freedom from it.

While e-cigarettes may make it a little easier to stop smoking tobacco cigarettes and some studies show a moderate advantage over the patch and gum, do you really believe these people want you to quit? Really? They are all drug dealers. Every one of them.

Beware of Dorffs Baring Gifts

Claudette Colbert circa 1942, dressed as a nurse passes out Chesterfields to GI's during WWII.

Implications are smoking is safe because a nurse is handing them out like candy and it's American because the guys bringing down Hitler and Japan all smoke.

Fast forward to 2013, Lorillard, owner of Newport and Kent amongst other cigarette brands also owns Blu e-cigarettes and has recently returned to advertising.

Celebrity endorsements and television commercials rise from the ashes to promote, justify and encourage those addicted to nicotine to switch their nicotine delivery device over to electronic cigarettes verses the traditional tobacco cigarette.

Stephen Dorff and Jenny McCarthy have whored themselves out to Lorillard and joined in this new deception and virtual hedge against the declining cigarette industry. E-cigarettes, while supposedly "vapor" do contain carcinogens such as formaldehyde and acrolein. And while admittedly safer than a traditional cigarette, what will the long term effects be? No one really knows.

I find it HIGHLY irresponsible of any celebrity to hop into bed with any company or industry who has spent the last 90 plus years lying to its customer base, manipulating the addictive properties of its product and packaging its product to minimize the perceived risk. If you smoke a "light" cigarette, keep in mind, there's no such thing as "light" cancer. You don't get "light" emphysema and there is no "light" trachea.

Dorff, you're too cool for your own good. You and McCarthy over there are both being used by a company in desperation with years of experience in manipulation. Selling your soul didn't end well for Robert Johnson or Jerry Garcia. Both of those cats were way cooler than you so what chance you think you got? Get out now and step up.

Teens are picking these up because of you and the e-cigarette is becoming a gate way for traditional cigarettes. Is this the legacy you want to leave? 30 years from now will you be going into radiation therapy saying (assuming you're still with us and not another early departure caused by big tobacco)

"we all thought it was just vapor..."

The Five Stages of Grief In The Non-Smoking Section

The Kubler-Ross Model otherwise known as The Five Stages of Grief.

How will it apply to those trying to quit smoking?

The Kubler - Ross Model and Smoking Cessation

Otherwise known as The Five Stages of Grief, this is something you, as someone looking to stop smoking very well may go through. So far you have learned to see smoking for what it is, an incredibly dysfunctional relationship. Have you ever been in a bad relationship and said, "This relationship's going to be the death of me!"

Sure it's all tongue in cheek until you throw cancer and emphysema into the mix...

So, let's take a look at The Five Stages of Grief and see how they apply to not smoking any more.

Notice that I will not say "trying" and will not use the term "quit" when talking about not smoking anymore. If you've made it this far, hopefully by now, you get it.

Stopping Smoking and Grief

Elisabeth Kubler-Ross published a book in 1969. The book was called, On Death and Dying. A nice cheerful subject it is! All kidding aside, this book examined what a person with a terminal illness goes through emotionally as they approach the big day (death). She interviewed and researched over 500 patients on their way out and found that they all cope with the inevitable in a very similar way.

This is how she isolated and identified these five stages. Now what's interesting is that while these stages are all common, they are not necessarily going to be chronological. What's important here for us, is recognizing that they exist and then having the self-awareness to see where we're at. What stage are we in as we go through the process of not smoking anymore?

"But Dave," you ask, "The Five Stages of Grief are for people who are dying from a terminal illness! What does this have to do with me? I'm just trying to quit smoking!"

Glad you asked! Your first problem is you're "trying" and your second problem is you're "trying to quit." Thirdly, odds are really good that smoking will lead to YOUR premature death so you better start coping now! And while we're at it, smoking *is* a terminal illness, let's face it.

OK, where was I?

Ultimately, as further research was done and time passed, it became clear that you don't have to be in the midst of a terminal illness or literally in a stage dying to experience this. People experience grief. Period. They have loss, tragedy, break ups, illness, etc. and one way or another people need to find a way to cope with what's happening or with what just happened.

Cope. That's the key word here. Dictionary.com defines "cope" as: to struggle or deal, especially on fairly even terms or with some degree of success (usually followed by "with")

Is it finally time for you to stop smoking? Transitioning to the non-smoking section will require some work. Let's examine five things you might go through along the way. Keep in mind you may be in one of these stages right now...

Denial

Denial ain't just a river in Egypt as they like to say! This may be rather obvious, or not, if you're in denial!

This is for those of you who are in the old, this doesn't apply to me, category. Just because Sammy Davis Jr, Nat King Cole, Humphrey Bogart, Spencer Tracy, Rod Serling, Jack Webb, Patrick Swayze, and countless others all died of smoking related illness, I'll be fine!

"It won't happen to me, I can quit anytime I want."

Edward R Murrow was 57 when Lung Cancer took him. Do you really want to check out at 57? He was quoted as saying, "I doubt I could spend a half hour without a cigarette with any comfort or ease." He died two days after turning 57.

This is denial folks. If you still think you'll be fine, if you still think cancer or other smoking related illnesses don't apply to you, you're either Wolverine from the X-Men or in denial. Which one is it?

Anger

"Why do I have to stop?" "This is bull$#!7!" "How can something so good be so bad?" "I should be able to smoke any damn where I please!" "Who are you to tell me what I can and can't do with my body?!?!?!"

As you can see, we're transitioning out of denial, starting to recognize that smoking cigarettes actually IS bad for you and that continued use will lead to your early demise. This anger phase my also resurface during withdrawals as well. You want to be extremely aware of this so as not to misdirect the anger in the wrong direction. You wouldn't want to unleash on some poor undeserving soul, that's not cool! Think spouse, kids, boss, 225 pound amateur UFC fighter...

In Wikipedia it says this, "Once in the second stage, the individual recognizes that denial cannot continue. Because of anger, the person is very difficult to care for due to misplaced feelings of rage and envy."

Two things to consider here. This is about you caring for yourself (finally) and so YOU need to be aware of your anger about stopping and give yourself permission to not only experience the anger but to find a way to filter it into something positive. Otherwise you wind up turning in to Darth Vader. (he needed a breathing apparatus. Coincidence? I think not!)

The other consideration here is the envy. You're going to have a few friends who will continue to smoke. Do not allow yourself to envy their continued self-destructive behavior. Instead, strive to make them envy you for having the strength to conquer this addiction. Believe you me, you have the strength!

Bargaining

What if....?

So when you're getting a handle on the fact that this relationship is "toxic" and that you need to stop or have already stopped and are trying to justify having a cigarette, you start bargaining with yourself and or your higher power.

Examples of this would be:

- I'd walk a mile for a Camel
- What if I can get down to just 5 a day?
- It's been 3 days, let me just have one now and I'll be alright
- God, if I can keep smoking, I'll go to church more often
- I'll only smoke at work
- One last cigarette and that'll be it!

You're postponing. You're trying to weasel out of doing what must be done. Basically, what's happening here is, "I know I need to quit, but if I could just... [insert tit for tat here]

First of all, stop trying to quit and just stop already, secondly, the word but (not butt) essentially, diminishes everything that came before it and what came before it is usually B.S. anyway.

"I really like you, but..."

See what I mean? The time to stop is now. No deals with the Devil. It didn't work out so well for Robert Johnson or Jerry Garcia and look what it did to poor Keith Richards.

Buckle down and ride the wave. Once you're aware that you may start trying to weasel your way out of it, you will then be able to recognize it, acknowledge it for what it is and then make the choice to move beyond it.

Depression

"Forget it man, it's too late, I can't quit, I've tried, it'll never work, it is what it is, if I get the cancer, I get the cancer, at least I died doing what I love... besides, there's nothing really worth living for anyway and I don't really deserve to live a healthy active live anyway. Screw it..."

That's right, it's down in the dumps time. You ever get dumped? Break up? You ever loose someone or something important to you? Of course you have. Dysfunctional or otherwise, you've had a long standing relationship with cigarettes and you are losing a friend right now. Being sad, missing it, these are quite normal feelings to have and there's no need to fight them right now. Especially, when you have the presence of mind to, again, recognize what's going on right now.

If you got the sadness on you, know a few things:

1. Your brain has been chemically altered by nicotine. After a couple days without any, you're body and mind will start returning to normal and that means your brain chemistry will change too, so being a little down right now makes since.
2. You can choose whether or not you are going to allow yourself to wallow or rise up.

Do not fight the depression. Fighting depression could very well be why you started smoking in the first place. Recognize that the mere act of stopping is an act of love and you're taking better care of yourself and this is part of a transition. It's not forever.

How to Stop Smoking in Nine Words: ***"I can't do this, but I'm doing it anyway."***

Acceptance

"I'm going to get through this; it's going to be OK."

Freedom is another word I like here. When researching this, I came across an idea that I loved. I found that The 5 Stages of Grief were also being acknowledged as a learning process.

Getting into the non-smoking section is also a learning process. You're learning how to live without nicotine in your life and you're learning new ways to deal with your circumstances other than smoking. You are not only coming to terms with not smoking, but you are learning how to live differently. Even the way you drive home will change. You get to find new ways to function in the car and you have a new route home, meaning you don't need to pop into 7-11 for a pack anymore, you can just go straight home.

This process will have an ebb and flow to it. There will be good moments and some pretty crappy ones too. The key principle here though is to commit to moving forward.

If you're rowing out to sea, you will have to fight the waves first. This will be the hardest part. Then the tide, also difficult, but not impossible at all. Soon you'll have the current to deal with and then you'll have just the ebb and flow of the sea.

Remember this though; you're the one rowing the boat! Take ownership and responsibility for where you row. The current may sway you, your job, your mission, your duty to yourself and to those who love you is to stay on course!

And so it goes... Light yourself up!

What stage are you in?

Do you like the idea that not smoking is a learning process?

Does that it make it even more tangible to you?

Smoking ultimately is a decision. You chose to start, now choose to stop! Don't quit. Don't "try" to quit.

Your opportunity is to learn to be a non-smoker. Learn to live your life better. Learn to love yourself better. You learned to walk, talk, tie your shoes, use a toilet. You learned to read and write, you learned to drive and at some point you learned that when certain things happen, both good and bad, that a cigarette goes quite well with that.

Now it is time to learn that you don't need a cigarette during those moments, learn that you can function without them, learn that you, not nicotine, is in control of your world. It's a process. Are you up for it?

www.ingramcontent.com/pod-product-compliance
Lightning Source LLC
Chambersburg PA
CBHW070756100426
42742CB00012B/2152